DÍA DE LOS MUERTOS

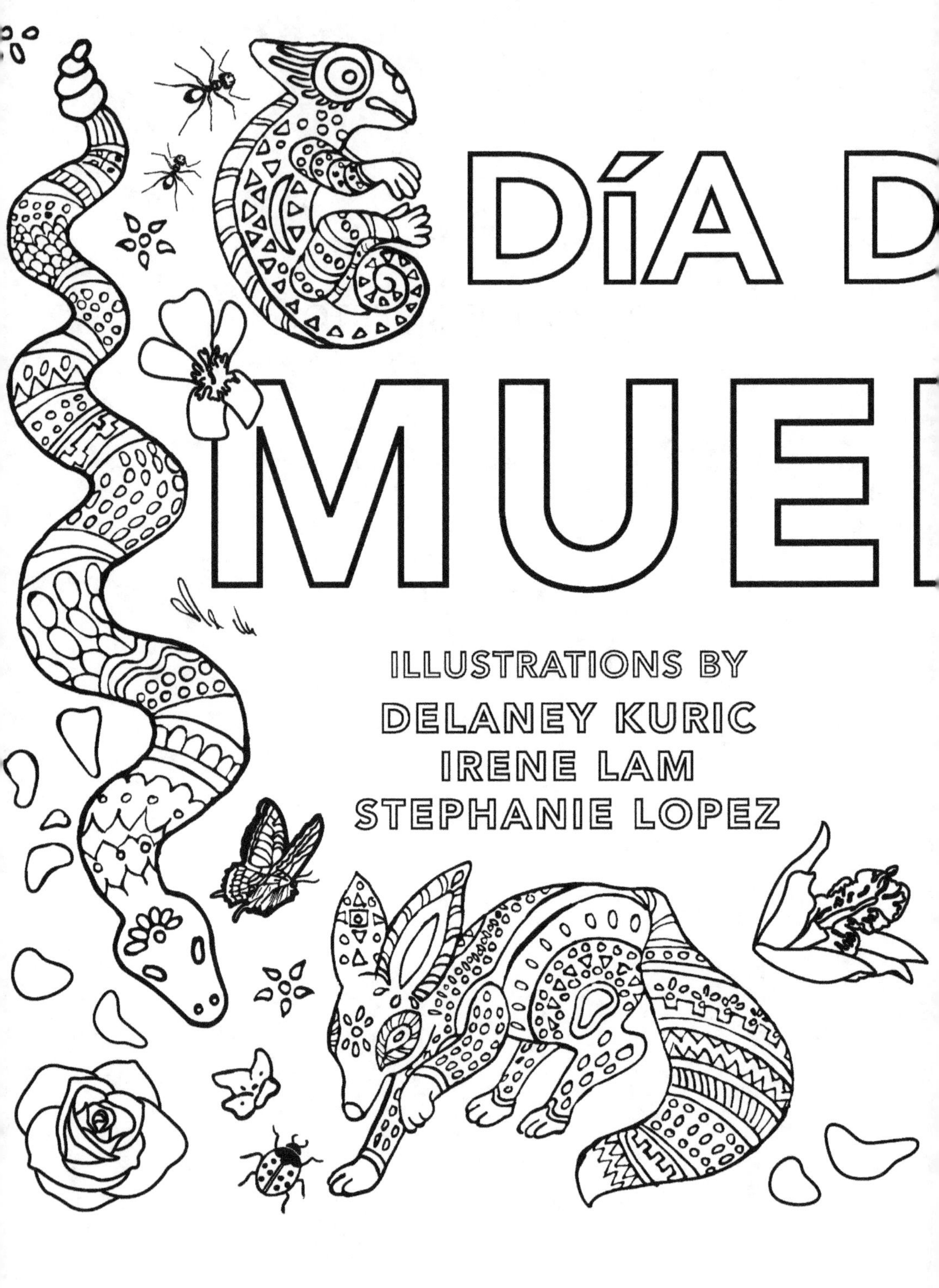

ILLUSTRATIONS BY

DELANEY KURIC

IRENE LAM

STEPHANIE LOPEZ

E LOS
RTOS

POEMS BY

GARY LEMONS

Red Hen Press | *Pasadena, CA*

Día de los Muertos

Book design and layout by Cassidy Trier & Selena Trager
Illustrations by Delaney Kuric, Irene Lam & Stephanie Lopez

Library of Congress Cataloging-in-Publication Data

Names: Lemons, Gary, author.
Title: Dia de los muertos / Gary Lemons.
Description: First edition. | Pasadena : Red Hen Press, [2016]
Identifiers: LCCN 2016030684 | ISBN 9781597097345 (softcover)
Subjects: LCSH: All Souls' Day—Mexico—Oaxaca (State)—Poetry.
Classification: LCC PS3612.E475 A6 2016b | DDC 811/.6—dc23
LC record available at https://lccn.loc.gov/2016030684

The National Endowment for the Arts, the Los Angeles County Arts Commission, the Los Angeles Department of Cultural Affairs, the Dwight Stuart Youth Fund, the Pasadena Arts & Culture Commission and the City of Pasadena Cultural Affairs Division, the Ahmanson Foundation, and Sony Pictures Entertainment partially support Red Hen Press.

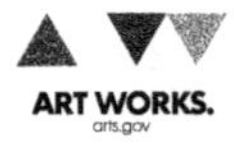

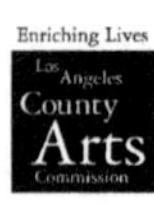

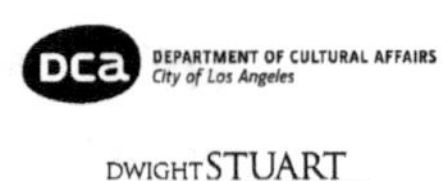

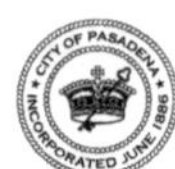

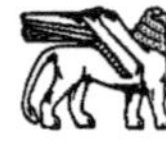
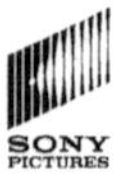

First Edition
Published by Red Hen Press
www.redhen.org

Día de los Muertos is dedicated with gratitude

to W. Nick Hill

for his wisdom—expressed in two tongues—
and for his friendship

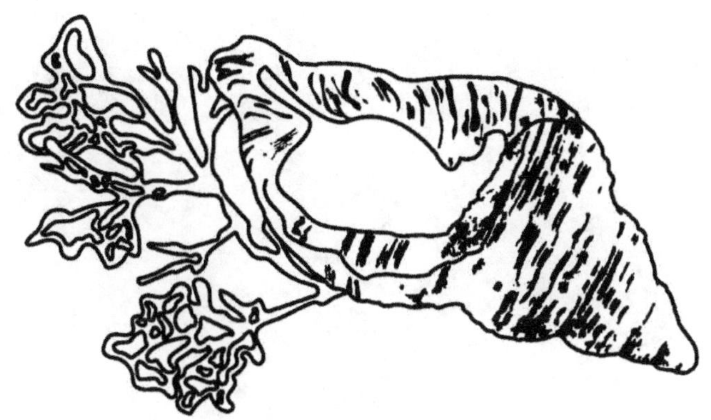

For Nöle

Forever

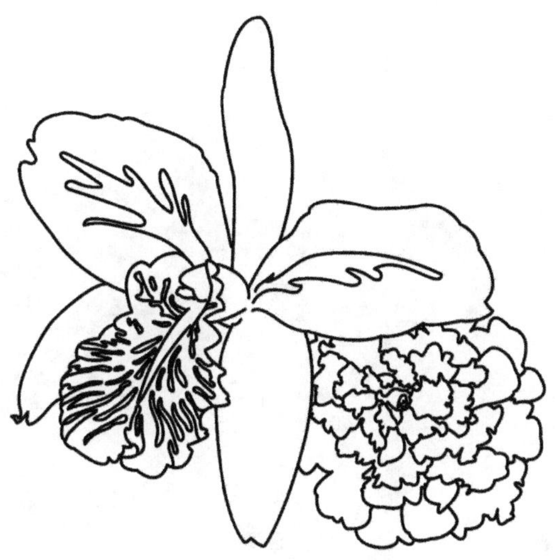

CONTENTS

DÍA DE LOS MUERTOS

AUTHOR'S NOTE

I spent a lot of time in Mexico from the late '60s through the early '80s. Once I spent almost a year in and around Oaxaca and was there twice for the celebration known as Día de los Muertos or, in the United States, Day of the Dead.

I was young and had no money saved. I worked cutting firewood, pouring concrete, or, as a mason's apprentice, building with brick and stone. When I had enough money I went to Mexico. I traveled with a backpack and a sleeping bag and slept in small hotels or rough on beaches and in forests. Sometimes I was invited into families and stayed a while helping out where I could. Sometimes I traveled with a partner but mostly alone. I walked beside burros loaded with sticks. Helped pull old trucks out of flooded rivers. Chopped cane with a machete, survived two scorpion stings, and learned to drink *pulque* with dignity. When I ran out of money I went back to the States and looked for work.

In retrospect I was living the life of a caricature. The young poet dissatisfied with ordinary local events looking for new experiences and sensations to serve as an incubator for images and perhaps revelations unavailable at home.

And I found them. I wandered through the Mexican landscape like a scrawled figure in a child's drawing. I walked the streets at night during Día de los Muertos in different cities at different ages and was touched by ancestors, licked by unfriendly witches, painted black by spooky grandmothers, exsanguinated by moonlight, and put back together by instructions from the worm in the empty bottles of mezcal. I danced with shadows that became real as soon as they touched me. It is no exaggeration to say those times in Mexico did more than any other spiritual practice or inquiry to convince me the dead are simply alive in a different place just outside peripheral vision.

Decades go by and I grow old and to my horror discover that yes—indeed—I wear my trousers rolled. Those days—those memories—sift to the bottom like sediment in a well.

Then one early morning in March 2015, something—a dream I believe—stirred the bottom and *Día de los Muertos* rose from that sediment. I sat down as I do every day with my coffee and started to write. Usually with no particular idea in mind—just waiting for something to come.

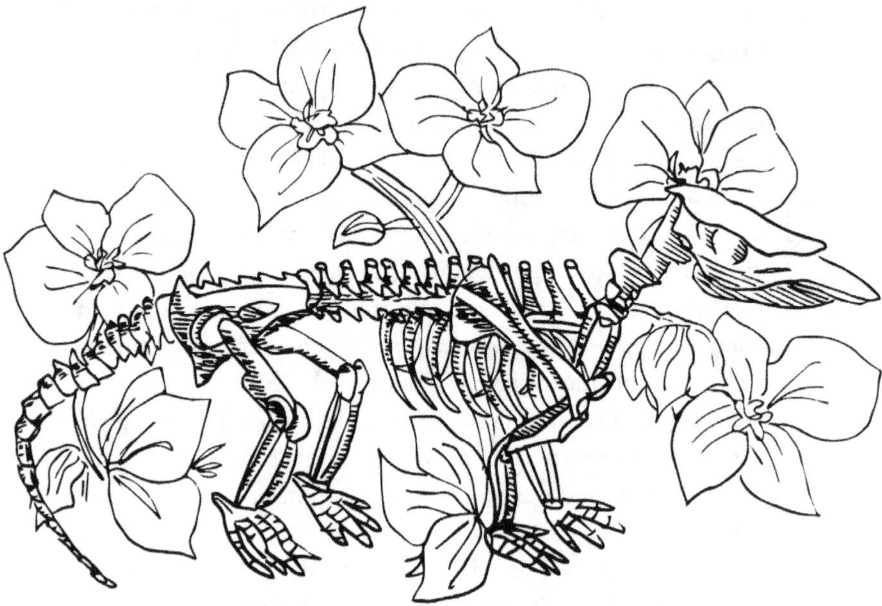

I found my way to Mazunte. To be in the same place sea turtles thought sacred enough to lay their eggs. I wanted to sleep on land that accepted this devotion to duty for a million years and welcomed it. I was unprepared for the carnage on the beaches when the turtles came ashore—and especially unprepared for the charnel house smoke that broke apart the air above the sleepy little town when the meat was cooked in the brick ovens. Outside the doors of the kitchens the colorless—hence unusable—part of shells were thrown into the dirt paths where over the years they solidified into a sort of dull white pavement. The first poem, "Mazunte"—which is really a preface—is a memory sifted from the rough granules of dream into the flour of the poem.

The last poem, "Borderline," is also a shifting, dream-like series of images embedded like fossils in the linguistics of text each of us carries in memory and which often is unearthed—either by intention or accident—as we move further away from it. Everything in my time in Mexico lent itself to the understanding that there are no real borders between things—not temporal and not physical—though the appearance of these differences—these places of disconnect—are reinforced from birth until at an early age we are convinced we are alone—each on the other side of an impermeable wall.

I caught a ride to Oaxaca just in time for Día de los Muertos. The afternoon after I arrived I was sitting in a small café at an outdoor table in the shade drinking freshly squeezed orange juice—the things you remember—when across the plaza an old deeply brown woman began to dance—not a choreographed move but a fluid ageless spinning around the axis of her sandals—and as she moved she cried out—*"de nada—de nada"*—over and over again. There were soldiers leaning against a wall also in the shade watching her and laughing but mostly people just walked by ignoring her. It was the last day of October 1969 and already under a harsh, unforgiving sun, the dead were staking terrain—moving in and around and through the apparently alive.

This book comes out of these events but decades have passed since then. Therefore the poems are not intended to be in keeping with the feeling qualities of Mexico today. The Mexico of today is—regrettably—a place I don't know. *Día de los Muertos* is—rather—like the bones of a giant beast dug out of a tar pit then reassembled. It must poorly represent the living creature.

The book still feels to me like the migration of a prayer or perhaps a curse uttered millions of years ago by the first creature misunderstanding the essential interaction between magic and mortality.

In *Día de los Muertos*, the occasional use of Spanish words or phrases occurred naturally and spontaneously as the poem was written. They were not afterthoughts but rather linguistic fossils left from a time when I was more fluent in that particularly beautiful and powerful variant of Spanish spoken in Mexico.

Also—the poems are divided into sections that were originally numbered. I look at these more like random encounters than sequential events. This is how it felt walking darkened streets beside strangers in painted masks or dressed as skeletons or actual skeletons or other strange and haunting figures—none of which are immediately believable or real—dancing and spinning around you—in and out of focus—with smells of cooked meat and cheap liquor and redolent bodies and sounds of horns and vihuelas and drums under a sky heavy with stars and streaked with ephemeral objects that in the moment look like attendant ghosts. These sections are then to be looked at as metaphorical encounters with strangers while running the spooky gauntlet of carnival.

Snake—the remnant voice of the collective in the Snake Quartet—entered this poem without intention. *Día de los Muertos* was written during the time I wrote *Snake: Second Wind*. In that snake is the repository for the dead and the living, it appears the insidious reptile was unable to abstain from cross-pollinating *Día de los Muertos*. Rather than resist I welcomed the additional reflections offered by her voice.

And the silence.
And the cities, sparkling, empty.
And the mediocrity, like a hot
lava, spewed out over
the grain, and the voice, and the idea.

—Rafael Guillén Vicente, "Not Fear"

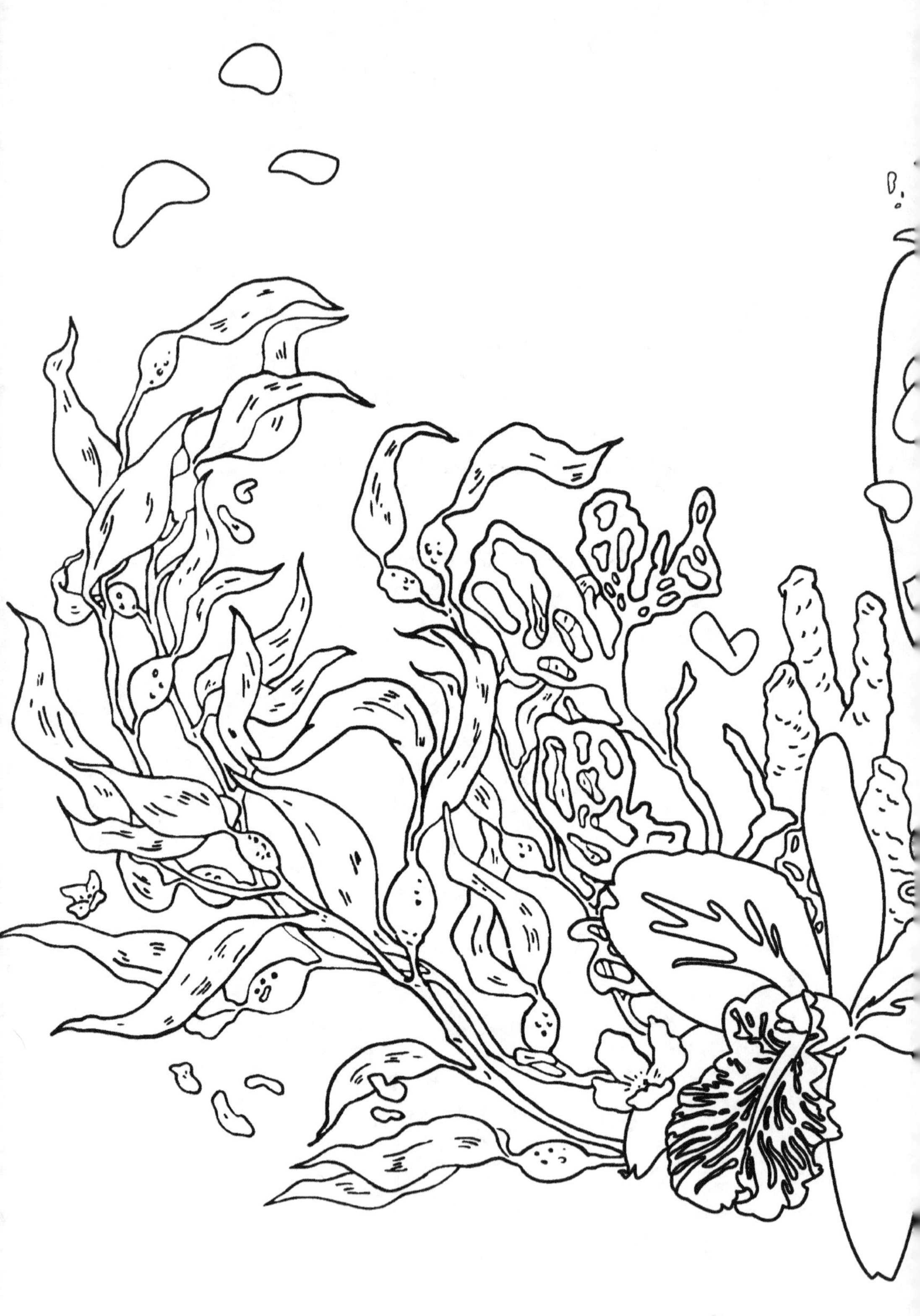

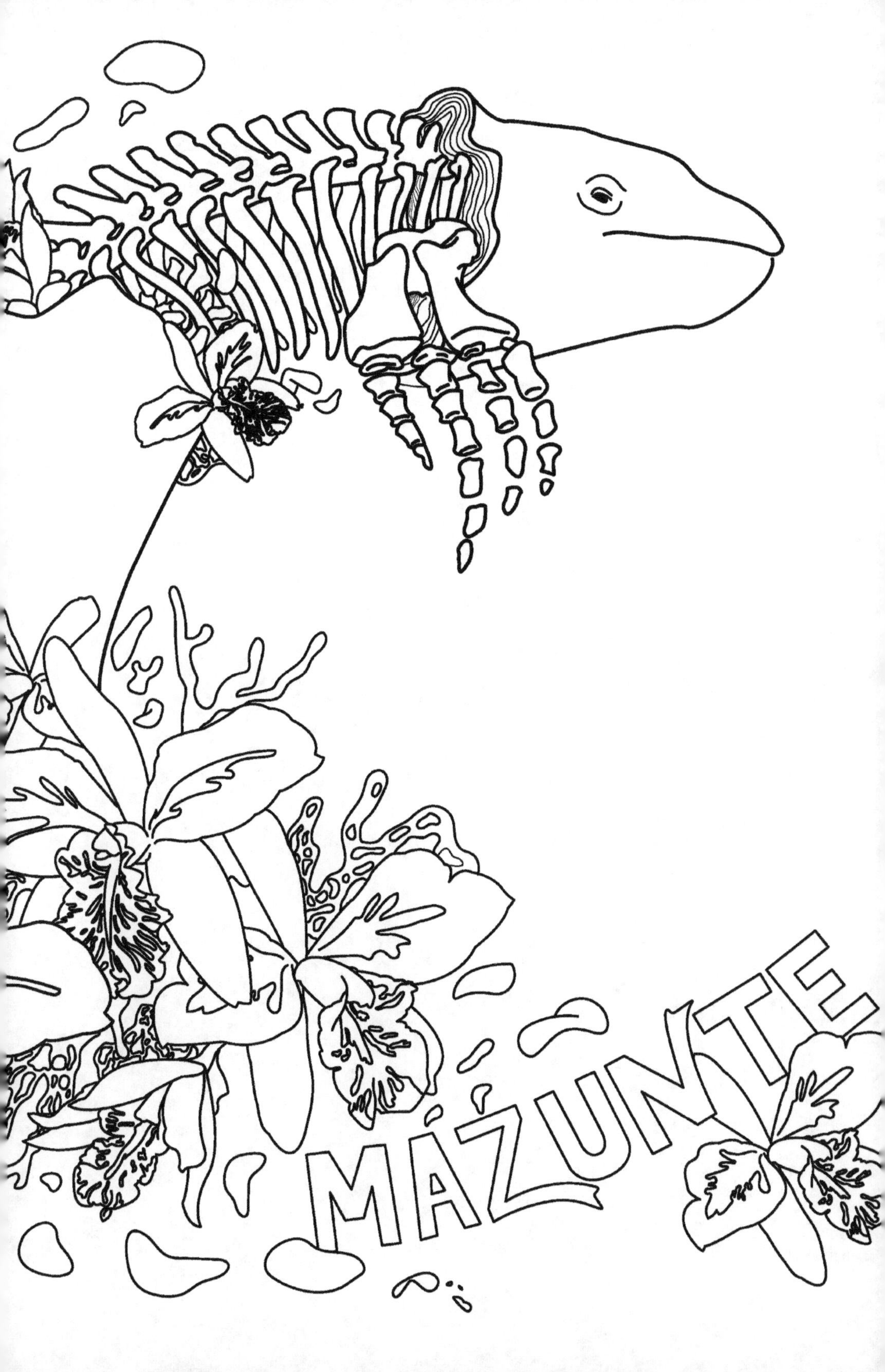
MAZUNTE

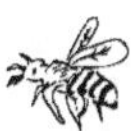

The smoke above Mazunte is greasy
Brown like a tubercular mist—it hangs from nostril
Hairs the way bats cling to pale crystals
In caves where their droppings asphyxiate
Lovers who come out of the sun to determine
Whether the consequences of lust—though
Different than those of love—are drained
By the same valves in the heart—

A single stroke and a coconut exhales
The overpowering scent of turtle meat—
I wake in the night beside a dead fire
To the quiet ministration of a hermit
Snapping fingers under my nose—the reek
Of bad lanolin and crevice—from the sea
A small determined creature crawls
As if between dreams out of a dark safety
Into the danger of creational light—

Overhead the sun pinches its nose
As it dives toward the adobe walls around
The church where children in black
And white uniforms exit squinting
Up at the sky for evidence the padre
Is telling the truth regarding the dispensation
Of favors in the kingdom of need.

The smoke from the brick chimney
Settles in the bowls of wet orchids.

I came here expecting the lagoon
To be this beautiful—a strange ellipsis

In which the burning tropical air hides
The smile of a cold northern goddess—
Blue eyed between the cavities of land
With white clarity and yellow glare—unrelenting
In the way its invasive stare punches
Through the half-closed eyes. The Viking
On this lovely beach rows in from the sea
With a passenger wrapped in fire
Who shouts her ice bound praise of darkness
At the shimmering gleam of broken shells
Left by the meditation of hammers.

Daylight is like this everywhere—
Bold and possessive with its hands
In your pocket looking for change
While it kisses you hard on the lips
Then turns you around with a slap

That sends you careening into evening
With its tongue still in your mouth.

It isn't exactly the huge flowers
Grinning like barkers at reluctant crowds
Or the taste of eels left from sucking
The roots of strangers in cantinas
Where the bouncers at the door keep
The abundance of light and its swaggering
Pastels from provoking the few customers
Hiding in dark booths like seals
Under ice looking up at white bears—

It's something like this—the abyss
Opening—the grateful absorption
Of water by a sponge—the grave waiting
Undug in the forest beneath the flying

Squirrels and trumpeting vines and shattered
Remnants of lost temples so much like privies
Behind fallen barns—the place ancestors
Left to ghosts who yet strain there.

Someone throws an anchor out of reason
And it splashes into the deep water of a promise
That waits another day for fulfillment—

Not today but yesterday—it is true
We are no longer adrift but stuck to liquid sky
In the lapis eyes of diaphanous life
Forms clinging to the rocks long
Enough to gasp prayers between tides—to
Both worship and despise a trembling
Savior shoveled out of the imagination
Of a creature hunted for its beauty as
Well as the taste of its afterlife.

In this land even the stones are thoughts—
Best not shared—waiting to be stacked
Into a wall around livestock.

But the smoke introduces the sad
Insight something right now is being cooked
Into paste as well as pressed between
Dried violets to turn the oils of its
Experience into a seductive cologne
For the freshly showered to cover
The odor from a rash.

The smoke of the dead turtles
Kills the light in the eyes of imported roses
Already struggling with coastal
Heat and hot condensations—the native

Blooms preen gaudily—sneeze
As if expecting an orgasm to follow—
While the roses—weary expatriates—
Bend to the ground and blush.

None of the local birds will come
To them—attempts at self-pollination fail—
Destiny appears to mark the place
Where prejudice begins—except thank god
For the callow bees who come bumbling
To the rose like toddlers to swings—

The old bees grumble in native blooms—
It's the season's gift there are always enough young
In the world to extract a tomorrow.

I lay in the driftwood wrapped
In a blanket with my ear against the sand—
Between the muffled thump and sizzle
Of the surf I hear witches synchronizing
Ardor into journey—the spells of one shy being
Swimming through the miracle of salt
In its blood—the expelled tears behind
Blindfolds finding their way to the sea—

All night my fingers and feet twitch
Like rags caught to brambles in the wind—
Like flippers directing a weight
Toward a light—like old age calling
From the island of a damaged tree—
The *arribada* has begun.

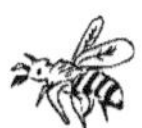

The roses speak with one voice
And I find it is also mine—entering
The dirty bar with the dirty man
In a bloody apron holding the head
Of a turkey in one hand and a beer
In the other—leering—yes—leering
As if his natural position was discovered
In the act of taking a life—like a saint
In fact—on the road to salvation
Not knowing who will arrive first—
The sin or the sinner or the screams
For mercy prodding every prayer
Into the marketplace to be sold.

Something in the dry palms rattles
Once like a gourd dropped by a child—
Tumbles to the sand and swims away.

This morning I slouch in the café worn
Out from a night imagining the slurry
Of bodies moving just below the surface
Of the sea the way dreams in daylight impede
And jostle old trucks in fast traffic—

There is a candy I ate as a child
With a hard crust of dark chocolate
Around a soft cherry—I remember
The resistance of the shape between
Molars before the burst of red light—
In the lagoon there are sharks
That right now I am surprised to find
Share this memory with me.

My feet are on the chair across
The table where someone
Later will sit and I'm unaware of the glances
Of the woman pressing fresh oranges
Who knows I am not from here
Because no local would be so rude.

The soldier sits down beside me
And stares with eyes liquid with camouflage
At my legs until I pop out of the doze
And carefully put my feet on the ground.

He asks me why a young blond
Gringo would come all the way to Mazunte
To die and I tell him I am not blond
And he assures me this is not the important
Aspect of his curiosity. When I say
To him that one is always making
A pilgrimage toward a disappearance—
He smiles and the ink in his eyes
Runs down his cheek to the napkin
Where it turns a certain amount of white
To black—the way faith will take hold
Of a child's wardrobe and make
A uniform—yes—he says—not blond.

This is the way I imagine
It is for those questioned
Endlessly in small cells in the back
Of their minds by prosecutors posing
As conscience—I fall asleep
In my chair—the pulp of the orange
Sinking to the bottom of the glass
Like the scales of fish to the ocean floor—

And in the bright shadow under
The rattling lapped palm fronds
I hear my snore—smell the last time I
Bathed—feel the movement of leathery
Fins in the veins of the blue Norse goddess
Who comes in the heart as the sea.

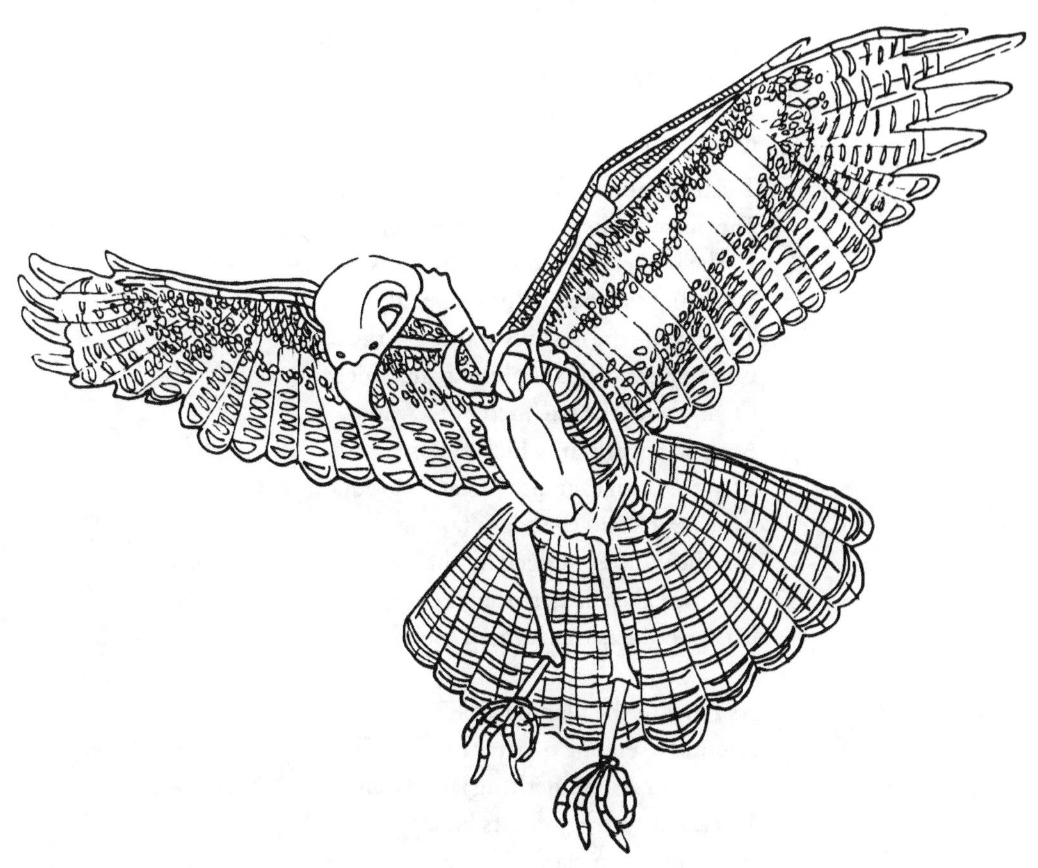

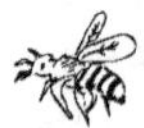

The hawksbill, the olive ridley, the green
And leatherback—the movement of tides,
The shifting of spectrums from horizons
Constantly reshaped by the effort to reach them—the
Tangible bite of shark or harpoon—the
Frets of the guitar worn down
By the fingers over the years—the sorrow
In the song—the waves—always the waves—
Drawing the fingers down the neck
Where the muscle is sweet and difficult—
The intimation of land beneath the shell—
The pulse in the sac—the hard eggs
In the basket—the doe in the forest
Straining as blood drips on needles—
The fawn—the coyotes waiting—the end
Of the light called night within which
Owls patrol the perimeter of a frame
Around a world in which chaos
Mingles with each heartbeat to produce
Mountains and the rocks falling
On the villages nudged by shadows
Too unreal to filter through pain or
To materialize in a human touch.

As I dream the planet revolves
Around itself one quarter turn while
In the nursery something rises from
Its cradle with eggs in its hands
And tiptoes on clawed feet out
The door into the bright light
Where it is erased by the soldier
Poking me with his pistol—saying
Gringo—you have slept in this chair
Where paying customers would sit

If you had not colonized it—and I
Slip some pesos under the bunched napkin
Beneath the now empty glass and thank
Him for allowing me the honor
Of making restitution for my sins—

He does not smile but blesses
Me and moves back into the shadows
With his small mustache wet
From drinking my juice.

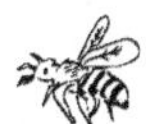

The moon is full tonight and I am gravid
With the generations to come in the way
A bell hangs for centuries contemplating

The beautiful tone it will make as soon
As collaborators arrive to strike it.

I am not unaware that my life
Has been longer than imagined—that
I have been rinsed free of belief
And given moonlight instead—

I am not unaware that the salt
In the water would punish my eyes were
It not for my beautiful design—
That—though I had no part in it—I
Celebrate in the dark recess of shell
Where a naked Saracen pounds its fist
Against a steel drum that ripples the blood
Like a comet burning into the sea—this

Driven vessel—swimming through tears
Toward harvest of broken shell.

There are journeys undertaken for
Known reasons but this is not one of those.
This is a journey I believe launched
From some original fire which is felt as thrust—
The manner of which is perfected
By whales who siphon ancient secrets
From deep water and reveal them again
In a plume of liquid Veda that turns
To nonsense when possessed by words—

If moonlight aligns with the crest
Of wave in such a fashion that splinters
Of far space—narrow as bone—white
As dead coral—come into my shell the way
The poor enter a shrine—on their knees—
The land whispers—*this way—this way.*

It is hard for a swimming turtle
To imagine these things but I assure
You—what is imagined by any of you
Is known to all of us—the stars are friends—
Sucked into the eyes like food so they
Travel deep into the places of instinct
Inside the dream where they fracture
Into diadems whose burning centers become
Directions the heart makes into maps.

I apologize for making this
More complex than it is—I am a simple
Turtle asked to address a superior
Species—drawn from a silent world
Into temporary being with a voice
Unfamiliar to my small tongue
By a memory so insistent it

Has successfully turned
The songs of coral into speech—

The mystery of this is yours—
Any truth that remains is mine—

If the dream is pleasant—meaning
If there is a night dark as a underwater eyes
And too little light for the hunters to see—
The sand soft and easily dug—the beach uncluttered by spears
Or clubs or the grunt and clack of beasts—
Then I will finish and go as you
Will finish and go home.

Perhaps if you are sleeping in a chair
In a sunlit café with shadows
Peeking out of vines like nestling
Birds waiting for the night to stuff
Them with stars—you will dream of a girl—
Or a boy—and someone will come
To you and their warm hands
Will take out your heart very carefully
To kiss it with great reverence.

And you will awaken swimming—

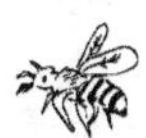

It is true that traveling rough—
Sleeping in clothing—eating small—
Dividing the days into siestas and weary
Trudging between holy places
With an unlit cigar in a pocket
Is one way to grow old—but many

Paths diverge from this moment
In which I find myself watching
An arthritic burro with pink ears yoked
To a handmade carousel plodding
In circles under the hot sun as the carved
And gaily painted animals turn
Slowly without riders while a group
Of children dressed in the black
And white uniform of the church walk
Beside the burro praying for it.

Why are they not riding the saddles
On the backs of the wooden beasts—why
Are they walking in this heat when they could
Enjoy the circular perspective not so different
From the faith of their fathers?

There is no one to answer this question.
The soldier has gone inside the café
And through the window I see him
Speaking fervently to a woman old
Enough to be his grandmother—if I read lips
I'm sure I would understand him to say
He is tired of the responsibility
Of cleaning a gun and is ready to lay down
In the sand and give birth to the mystery
No one wants alive in this world.

When I look around—one of the children
Is standing beside me with her hand out.
Inside her palm there is a peso she
Offers with the generosity of sunlight—
"*Por favor Señor*—for the price of a smile."

I ask her why the children don't
Ride the carousel and she explains

The donkey belongs to them
And it is their duty to treat it with
Respect and not burden it with the weight
Of their pleasure—she is a field
Of kelp at high tide—undulating
In the current of a magnificent force
That is all that keeps the carousel
From spinning into the cold, lonely
Reaches of dark and empty space.

I get up from my chair and walk
To the donkey and release the yoke
Around its shoulders—the sky
Is filled with whirling birds and the sound
Of the distant waves seem more
Remembered than real but if
I look to the west the ocean glitters
In the manner of a goddess with eyes so blue
The only escape is into her—

I take the yoke—covered
With short gray hairs and wet with sweat
And smells as lovely as a box of love letters—
And fit it to my shoulders—

Now the migration begins—it
Is enough the judgment of sunlight
Turns my hair blond and ignites Viking
Fires deep under the sea to guide
The turtles into each of us—I follow the well
Worn path around and around while
The children ride on the wooden animals
Laughing like bees in hot flowers—
The little burro rolls in the dirt—braying
Like a god suddenly released from
The weight of our unanswered prayers.

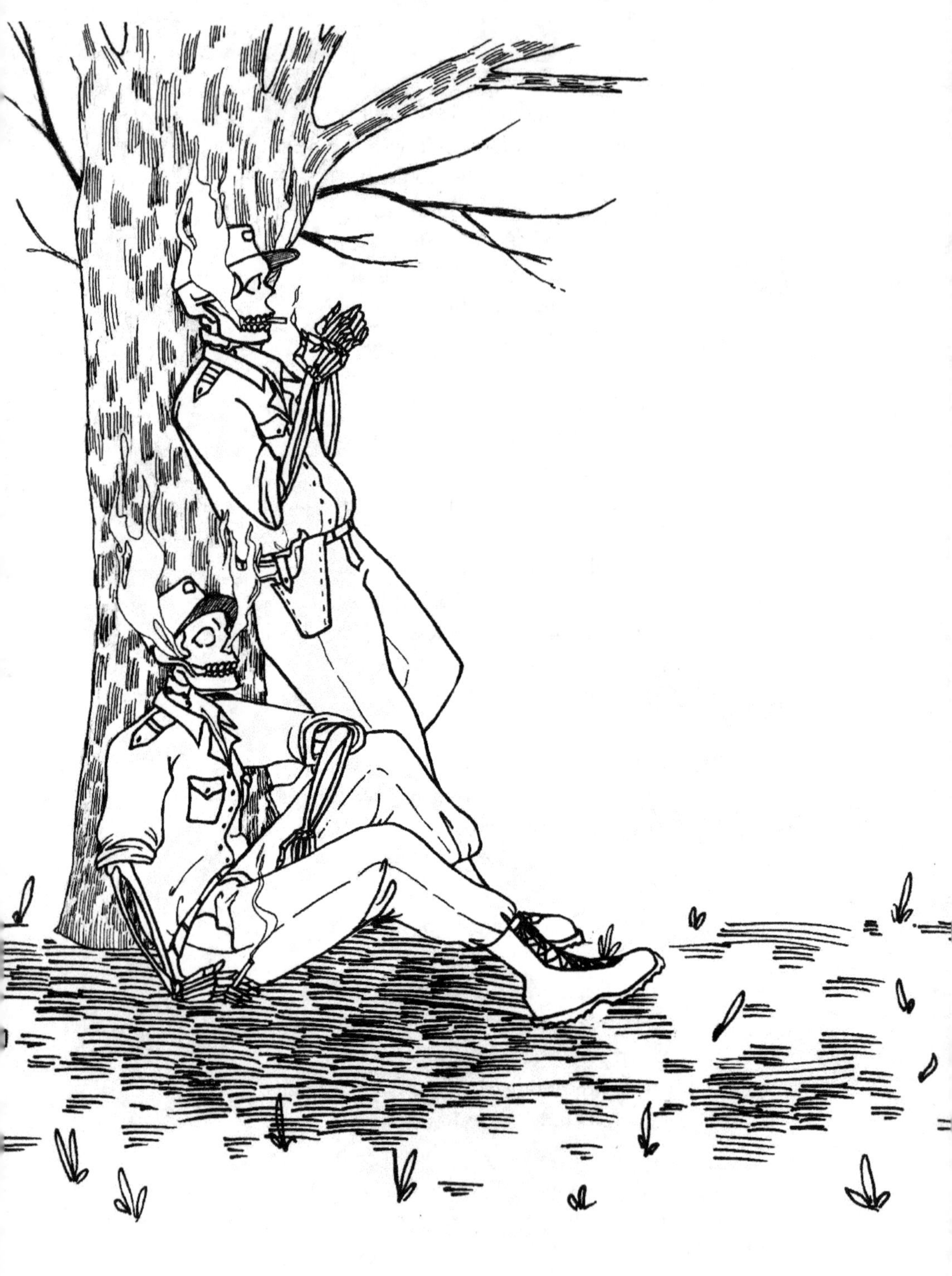

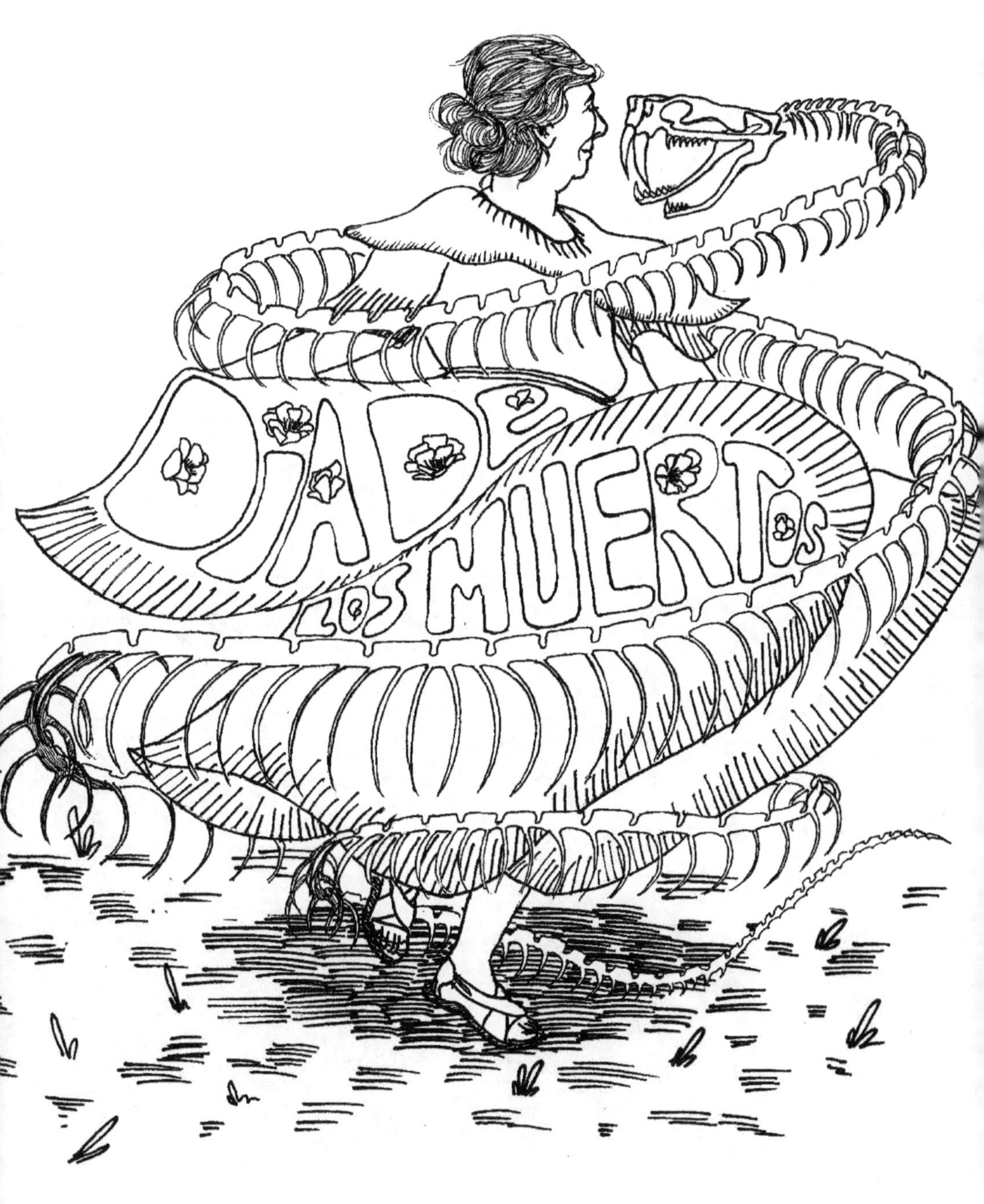
DIA DE LOS MUERTOS

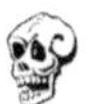

The old woman in trailing rags
Sprays *de nadas* around the empty square
Like spittle from the mouths
Of vaqueros panting in their saddles
At the end of a hard day's ride—

El hacendado notes their inadequacies
With a small downturn of the lip—tells them the bulls
Came back on their own—tired of wandering
Dried up summer pastures over flown
By solitary birds of prey—they came home
For food—for fresh water—wild and sick
From drinking the bitter green runoff
Beneath the arsenic mines that sparkle
Like melted emeralds in the sun—

Unfortunately they left their testicles
Behind—hanging pink and limp
From a neighbor's gate—like balloons
After fiesta—no longer engorged
With the breath of vendors—the cost
Of trespass in this merciless land.

She twirls slowly in the dust—
Becoming dust—as if bones in her body
Took up arms against her heart
And pierced vital organs to expel the hemorrhagic
Burst of wet roses falling one petal
At a time from the memory of a lover who died
On just such a day as this—without wind—
With soldiers in the shadows
Lifting armpits to sniff their fear—

But the day of the dead is arranged
So the living may momentarily touch
What will be taken in a mad scuttle toward
Relevance—may stumble—yet somehow
Not fall in the hole underfoot—

We walk up to it anyway—even though
The solitary bird flies away hungry
Its shadow follows us—this strange
Ventriloquism between horror and faith—

These messengers with roses in their
Teeth and electric eyes that love
Nothing more than to crawl in bed
Naked and pump us full of *la verdad*
In an attempt to wallpaper a scream—

Why do I return to the rose—
I forget—oh yes—because the manicured
Trellis with the holiday faces—so North
American in their way of owning
The air with color and perfume—
So fragile in the way even the gaudy
Ones succumb to mandibles—

Grow out of the stinking peat
At their feet—the bags brought
From the nursery with millions
Of bodies pressed by struggle in a luckless
Irish meadow churned by weather
And bog ponies—bags of dry whimpers
Sold to grow just such flowers
To excite the shears of the heart—

There is such a thing in politics—
Well disguised as plentitude—called power
By ordinary despots—mingled with spittoon
Dribble and grease from spatulated thumbs pushed
Into the ribs of secretaries chosen not
For their skills but for holes in their stocking—

To some these places where the skin
Shows through are also roses—
Finally—following the tracks
Of the bleeding bulls until the spoor
Dries up and merges with the dust
From the old woman's dance—men
Approach from the crease in the page—
Often called the horizon—with guns
And promises—both of which
They hope to use to possess the
Spirits the old woman conjures
From the ground with each sandal thump—

With each slow twist of her neck
She sees they are her brothers.

Truly she is getting younger
As the day dances into night—this
Is why the soldiers come—to
Make war against time—to throw rough
Sacks over precious hours and hijack
Them to lonely places beneath
The arsenic mines where—when enough
Are gathered—an excommunication
Of light from the eye occurs—

Which they use like brilliantine
To control the grizzled mustache hairs—

Everyone is celebrating something—
Even if it is not a time for celebration—
El chingado under the piled stone
Pulls the scorpion atop his loins
And floods a drying river—

The soldiers partake of the old
Woman by mincing in her steps until their dust
Mingles in the hot air with the dust
Of every person brave enough to stand
On their feet in front of god and shout the name
Of the lost child the vaqueros abandoned
In their search for livestock—

Finally the soldiers achieve their aim
And steal from *la bailadora* something they
Place upon a pedestal for target practice—

Something so beautiful it falls
Out of the mouth like a verb
Attaching itself to a sleeping lion—

A revolution of sorts inside the mouth
Where the words *I love you*
Form like a storm that damages
The fences but whispers green secrets
To fields enslaved by violent suns.
It is the utterance—not the contained
Thought unspoken—that dismasts
Men of war and causes bright origami
Storks above a cradle to spin
As if caught in a river of laughter
Flowing into the newly born—
Here is the center of ferocity—
Here the morning-after shot of tequila is

Taken directly from the monstrance
Before a secular confession—
Made with good intention but—
Unfortunately—false once uttered—

Is rescinded in the enamel fields—
Having lost the tracks of the wandering
Bulls—the vaqueros gather around
The scarecrow hung from an upright pole
Like a ragged man on a playing card
That survived the wind only to be torn
Apart by the undivided attention
Of gods that mistook it for the creature
They put on earth to kill—

All anyone can do is stop praying—

(*here it might be interesting—*
though there is so little time—to speak
of the two Mayan boys—the bold
ball players of Popul Vuh—not of course the balls
of the bulls or el chingado—but specifically
of their intercessor—a rat—who looks
them in the eye as they dangle it by the
tail over a cooking fire as it speaks sincerely
enough to convince the twins not to eat
it but instead become great players
in a game against the gods—

this is the story that causes the old woman
to dance as the soldiers approach—she is
invested with vermin—like all witches—and consequently
tells the future of each person who reads this poem
by plucking a metaphorical hair from their nose—
using it to divine in which universe the rat

hides the only map showing the way
out of the lost continent of epilogues—

whew—it is tiring keeping these fictitious
strangers from each other's throats
and for that reason alone I'll say
no more about the rat or the spectacular
victory the boys achieved against
the gods using their father's balls)

Oh yes—it is a day for intervention—
Withheld or offered it makes no difference—
For *solidaridad*—for mercy—for
No hay de que—for *chilaquiles* made
From the corpse of memories so shining
They swim in the sky long after the friars
Bottled the green water from the mines
And sold it to heal the damaged bulls—
Long after the earth and stars
Are gone—

Yes—the gods and the dead
And the living share the fruit cake
Delivered by horseback—a blue roan
With black mane and tail—seven
Generations ago by a grandmother
Who had no idea her dessert would be used
To hammer at least an apology from
The head of an unfaithful husband—

Let's include the patio furniture
Blown down by storms—(you see—
The storm that frightened the bulls
Into breaking free returns)—or
The children of the peasants pulled

From *el patrón*'s freezer and arranged
In a nativity scene so neighbors
Can see how the bosses celebrate
And honor their small losses—

Understand—today is for flying
Backwards into history—where we find
The futures of the unborn hanging
In orchards like fruit about to fall—

Today—as every day—is the day
To forgive *la niñera* who forgot
Children are unprepared to think
Of technical things like freezers
When their minds still believe
In the power of storks to ferry
Messages from angels momentarily
Lit up by gunfire above flowers—

Intervention—it comes in the form
Of a comet or a pointed boot
Or a feather duster to disrupt the current
Of order with different order—
Of a kind that leaves everything
Breathless—like skeletons
Waiting under a street lamp
In a mythological city shaken apart
Because its author was hung
Over and drank a second tequila
Before breakfast and decided—today—
This world I made from nothing
But the smile of a rose will end.

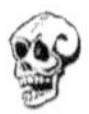

It is of course the willingness
Of the characters in any fictitious account
To believe their story is real that
Causes the freshly painted walls
Of the monastery to molder and peel—

For instance—the ship on the horizon
Is at first a tiny speck at which point
No one on shore understands that aboard
This vessel hides a legendary rat—(yes—
The same rodent who chewed fables
From the loins of the twin boys with
Incisors sharpened on the leg bones
Of minatory façades)—who comes
To guide the pack mules of apostates
To banquets in honor of the organ
They donate to the feast—

The rat is alone on the empty ship
In a small room with coiled

Hawsers and buckets of tar the color
And consistency of vampire hurl—

Here we are—agog at the dock
Cheering the ship's advance until
Someone in an adobe tower strikes a bell
Warning everyone to run—the ship
Is manned by ghosts come to occupy
Any body not fast enough to fall back
To the quiet room where the author
Sits with its evening sherry deciding
What to do with pages written during
A current bout of constipation—

The dead people alive in us
Are like this author—may be this author—
Straining all night with a glass
Of spirits in hand—editing
Boring story lines—throwing pages
In the fireplace causing it to flare
Like a momentary face in a window—

Keeping the good stuff—inevitably
The pain and mockery and disillusionment
Making the cut over mercy and reverence
And the hymn in every summer bee—

This is not the dead saying—forgive me—
This is the gods putting a rat in our mouth—or
Flowers left by enemies on a grave—

Okay—the ship arrives empty—
Indeed—the shore is also empty—
It is the untitled page—as yet
No decisions have been made
About what to call the child
Howling while shadows smack
Its wrinkled bottom into life—it
Is enough the child overlooked by
The vaqueros is returned to the poem
With one breath remaining—

This is when snake appeared—
Not in some paleolithic seam of humid jungle—
Not in the pockets of an orphan
Returned by foster parents for
Peeking at *los fornicarios* through keyholes—
But out of what would be called
Thin air—except that it's air peopled

With heavy inevitable matter like the faint
Fragrance of winter roses and
The dead and the unborn held in the
Same fist as a sharp stone—
And—of course—the rat—which is
The closest available hidden panel
Into the subjunctive gods—

Someone brings the author
Another sherry—one too many thinks
Snake—knowing the effects stimulants
Have on anything impaled on a thorn—
Which is the title of the new
Edition of every unwritten tomorrow—
Shortened—thankfully—to—
Adiós.

Upon downing the last glass
The author lights a candle—slowly—
Because its bones are old and not real—
Climbs the staircase to the familiar
Bed—blows out the candle—and just
For a moment—the dead and living
Curl together in a prenuptial embrace.

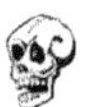

It is in the dark—with no
Sensation other than irritated
Membranes—where faith hides
Like infamous words within
A beatific expression—such as
I love that you are gone—it is
Often a small kindness that

Blots the sweat from the faces
Of those who hike the rough—
Wasted land where human
Kindness is rare as a full canteen—

Governments have no loyalties
Other than to the dead—which is
Why the living must die to get
What they need—a truce
Of sorts in which depravity
And fear remain beneath the jaws
Of desert lions while something
Free makes increasingly larger circles
To break from its need to also
Feast on the suffering place—

We are allowed to believe
The night is over and we
Are still real—even though
The author rises and goes
For the day—his unmade bed
Is soiled and we see how filthy
The body that before now
Seemed so immaculate.
Oh to live in yesterday, today
And tomorrow all at once—but think
Of the bitter custody suit for
This remaining breath—

It is true—where there is only
Wind ordinary things like paperweights
Are considered holy—
There was a time when no
Sombreros in the marketplace
Were made in China—a hat

Made by the grandfather passed
To the son who gave it to his—
The sweat on the band proudly
Displayed like an honorable wound.

Where the best grasses are found
Was a closely guarded family secret—
Like the rapture of a mute child
Or the infidelities of *el patrón*—
Talked about but only in whispers
Between the ones slicing meat
From the splendid bones of the beast—

Now there are men on horseback
Wearing sombreros made
Of Yangtze river grasses which smell
Of carp and become brittle
And break under a desert sun—

There are import tags on everything—
Even the kiss given like a novena
By teenage girls to shy boys.

The blue roan alone swishes
Its black tail and stands on legs
Firmly planted on both sides of a line—
Waiting for a rider dead enough
To deserve the journey it offers.

If our pain was ever sufficient
To truly keep our avarice under control
Then our greed could not be
Contained and like bears—insensible
To a million stings—we'd tear our
Ancestors from the living hive.

The dead see everything
On this—their day—which the living
Understand belongs to them as well—
Why else walk to the graveyard
Under boiling autumn clouds smiling
At the skull in each other's face—
Carrying our bones inside our skin
As if bringing a holy relic to the kitchen
To worship in a frying pan.

Where is the cemetery for myth?
Where do we bury the characters
That enthrall children as we
Grow old and forget them—who
Stands with limp prayers and a fresh
Lily beside a vertical stone
Mumbling *padre nuestro* until
The words fall to the grown
And darken mushrooms that
Wizards pull from the soil with
The sound of a disjointed bone to
Help them understand the power
Of death is doubled by resisting it.

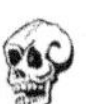

Two muscular twins roll out of bed
After sharing a dream where they win
A great victory over the gods
By killing them then giving them
Back an aquatic life inside a tear—
Outside their window the bulls
Drip blood down the inside of

Back legs as they return to the barn—
Dirty—empty—walking past the herd
With no interest in the heifer's stance—
While the blue roan stands on
A hill overlooking the hacienda
Like a hood ornament on an old Packard
Truck driven by a wealthy blasphemer
Of the saddle—I suppose it is
No longer correct to call them bulls.

From this dream—felt like
An icicle shoved between the ribs
Into the heart—melting along
The way until only the remains
Of winter enters the ventricle—

The gods understand the world
They made is no longer in their
Control—their creations are
No longer in awe of them and in fact
Are approaching with shears
Like florists toward a rare
But carnivorous blossom blushing
The limpid pink of its meal—

On the balcony of her bedroom
On the third floor overlooking
This garden where mortals and gods
Pluck one another with
Various tools such as death
Or disbelief—a celestial being
Never seen before within any
Bona fide rendering of the eternal
Kingdoms of life or death—gets up
From the banquet in her sister's bed—

Stares at the distant sea the color
Of the blue roan's eye after it
Is mounted by sunlight—sees

The ship is coming closer—
The mythical figures are thrown
Overboard—the rat is now
Celebrating under water
With those who revere a dropped
Anchor—no one is in charge
Anywhere—especially under
The sombreros of the sons
Or the mantillas of the daughters—
Only Sísifo—with a dull knife
Following the last bull that escaped
The ceremony of atonement—

This is because no one is alive
Anywhere—or—to say it properly—
No one is dead anywhere—

There are only these elemental
Needs in search of a bone
To animate the ongoing struggle
For dominion over the ecstasy
Of loving what comes and goes—

It is the surprising solace
Of mortality that allows forever
To hang upside down in its cave
And sleep all day until the night
Comes again and it feeds on
Its selves that fell to the floor.

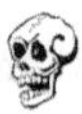

We celebrate Día de Muertos—
I know—the dead tell us this with
Every apostrophe the author
Throws between bodies to explain
The next possession—while
Others mourn our passing we
Are waking in a barn that smells
Of fresh cut hay—blood under
A lifted tail and the ivory bellies
Of swallows flitting at the edges
Of *comprensión* like the voice of fire
In the minds of bound Cistercians
Opening their mouth for the first
Time in centuries to release
The genitals of unbroken silence—

This awakening after death
Is an unknowable—unbelievable
Gift from the bog ponies that
Help prepare the ground for roses
And the evacuation of spirits
By their own evacuations—

Suddenly the breath stops
In the way of storms—for a moment
It is time to assess what remains—

Snake—awake at the wheel of a giant
Cart hurtling down a narrow mountain
Road—her sombrero of Yangtze
River grass and the smells
Of carp incite the blue roan pulling

Them faster toward a misperception—
Awake to the grinding sound of a wheel—
Shaped by a young mother whose child
Is missing—falling off—a spoke shattering
Like the tibia of a bull caught in
Barbed wire—thumping like the sandals
Of an old woman dancing
In the dust of a village square—
Expelling *de nadas* from her lips
To collide in midair with birds of prey who
Glide through bloodless afterlives—

It is a requirement of canonization
To dance in plain view of the lame
Of foot stuck in their seats by
Moral uncertainties regarding the expression
Of joy and decay of bone—to
Understand that demons are simply
Poorly chosen chaperones who
Sniff their fingers at the end of every
Performance—who live without reverence
Inside the architecture of brides—

Who—so far from their duties—
Escort the newly wedded shadows
To a place where vendors blow
Up balloons with a mezcal breath
So virile it inserts a worm in
Each balloon they fill—who
Read the palms of farmers
To foretell futures of those who wander
The mercado after the dance—before
The stalls close—looking for bargains—
Or promises covered with more flies
Than a hanging leg of goat—

The skill to clearly translate
The Aztecan gods into modern languages
Is the only requirement for the occupation
Of demon—otherwise they are
Just like you and me—

Snake gets out of the cart—
Not to change the wheel—it is
Beyond repair and there is no spare—

To walk for a while in the woods
Beside this lovely fatal road—
To sniff the ditches for possible meals—
Hoping another vehicle will offer
A ride—enjoying the freedom
From work called rigor mortis
By those on the other side
Of the dirty window—listening
For the dead as they approach
Like raptors into bullet-
Proof glass—singing until they're hoarse—
(please do not suspect any influence
Over this stanza by the blue roan)—
Until their voices turn to the
Music of rain below ground—

Until they sing no more—until
They slow down like a sundial defaced
By weather and centuries measuring
So many untimely deaths
It becomes a perch for the moon—

Snake's mouth fills with silence—
Like the living—like the dead—

Like the celebration of song in every
Fossil—under each stone—her

Mouth fills with a feast of silence
Which tastes like a mist of cradles—

That is gently metallic like the rings
Of Saturn and tastes of the watch-fire
In a fist at the end of a bodliless arm.

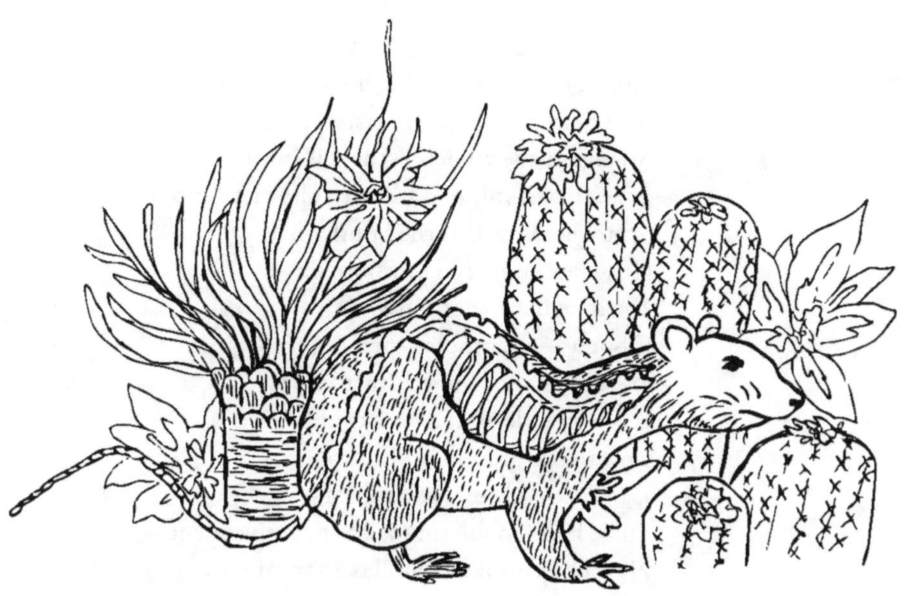

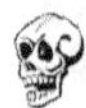

Children fear the bones
That walk without flesh—

Speckled by dust motes and light
Through broken walls in falling barns
Where grandfathers hang unfound
For decades after bankers repossess
The tractors and the dream—

Adults learn to love the bones
But fear what grows around them—

There are characters the author
Considers adding to the plot in the way
A two-fingered urchin masters all five
Strings of the vihuela—there is infinite
Space in the mind to fill with alternatives to
Strangers as well as the family that
Grows around each footnote in
The imagination of birds
Of prey—or authors—picking words from
The ossuary for something to love—
It is easy to look at a dust cloud
Low to the ground in the brown
Distance and see what appears
To be bulls copulating with the resplendent
New flowers on the chollas after rain—

The vaqueros sleep beside
Hobbled horses—on thin blankets
Wrapped in greasy ponchos after a day
Of whetstones—who can blame them if

They are too tired to prevent the original
Ghosts of this land from eating
The fire as they dream of sons
With aristocratic hands—

On this field every horizon—
Every page—every leaning tree
Or dry creek or tongue of monster begins
A secession—not unlike a civil
War where relatives take pleasure
In personal increase through killing heirs—
Begins a pirouette away from
The narcotic light inside a thorn—

Here for instance is a skull—
A fine horned palace flensed
By blown sand and empty of greed
Or love or lust or desire for water—

It is the skull of the bull the author
Forgot—the one that remained a bull—
That did not come back with the others—
Escaped early in the story—before the epilogue
Emerged from the ball sack kicked
By the mythical twins beyond the reach
Of the gods responsible for protecting
Other gods from human infections—

Before the author became obsessed
With the lizards sunning in verbs—
Back when free speech was respected
Much as an honest carpenter walks
Safely among trees—when freedom
Was no more than a noun in a dress—
An honorable way to elevate

The dust into shadows that eat the worms
Inside the bottled songs of the dead
And spit them into bassinets—

Inside the dance hall of the skull
Flies buzz with the intensity
Of thought—they are trying to
Get the skull to grow a new tail—
Trying by their ferocious noise
To animate the bone—the ceiling
Of this desert shrine—to break out
In beautiful thoughts such as one feels
Looking at the pulsing veins in a wrist—

Or when articulating a perfect
Rose from a peat bog with hard work
Transporting shot glasses of rain—

The bull is not going to think thoughts
Or grow a tale ever again—it is too
Late—but that doesn't mean the flies stop
Buzzing inside the empty skull—or the tiles
Of the magnificent ruined palace don't
Still ring with the jester's laugh—hah—
That would mean the ball game was decided
In favor of those who applaud each time
The twins score by breaking off fingers
And leaving them on the field—

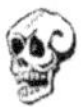

Notice—says *el patrón*—
My cook prepared this banquet
In your honor with all your
Favorite things—for the vaqueros—
A sorbet of starlight topped
With cherries like a campfire—for *el chingado*—

There is *pene del macho cabrío*
In a broth of saddle sores—what's this—

You want the sorbet?
Then let go of yourself and ride—

For *el escorpión*—who came to my wife
In the guise of a magician with moist
Lips and gigantic bulges—
Hah—yes—it was me—there are
Pesos from the shredder
Covered in blood and baked
Until crisp as a serving wench—

For the priest here is the wooden
Leg of a foundling child carved into figurines
That bleed—soaked in enough pain—
(we sacrificed a hen in its presence)
To allow the taste to sharpen like
Cheese from a bullock's thigh)—

For everyone there is something
At this banquet—except—noble
Peons and elevated cysts on my rump—
There is no tequila—no mezcal—

No *pulque*—the author forbids it—
Only this ancient wine made from
The dreams of ancestors who never
Imagined we'd be so far apart
And still in this world—together—

Enjoy! Someone died for this
Toast I offer—that your sons grow
Less bold and your daughters
Bolder every year.

Outside the oracle in the branches
Of the last deodar cedar tree
Is not a beautiful bird or plumed
Serpent singing of the inherent
Loveliness in every setting sun—
But a bearded old *mirón*
With his foot caught tight
In a notch shouting in the fragrant
Limbs the implications of his secret
Knowledge of servants—mistresses—
And *el escorpión's* implant.

If he raved like this on the ground
His message would be dismissed
As the anchorite is dismissed
By school children waving red
Scarves where two roads converge—

Because he shouts from so high
No one can see him—his prophecies
Are taken seriously—his suffering—
Retains a status usually given to hurricanes
Or the oracular clippings off a corpse—

El patrón is a simple man—
He asks his vaqueros to cut
Down this last tree looking in
At his bedroom with the mad *mirón*
Near the dark trunk—then continues
To butcher his livestock with words.

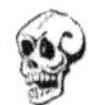

The day of the dead ends
When the night begins—when
The skeletons of horses find
Skeletons of riders—they ride—

The time comes to chisel tears
From the wooden faces of saints—
The curled shavings wetting the dirt
Floor of a young mother shaping a wheel
On a child's wagon—she
Listens to the mockingbird
In the cracked adobe tower outside
Her shed where an old woman
In a rebozo dances to its
One note—a duet between
Lovers where both move nimble
Fingers on a ligament or string—

Overhead the sun
Summarizes with a procession of
Hanging balls the daily game the living
Play to love the dead—

A mockingbird is not a bugle
So the soldiers in the shadows
Watching the old woman augur
With her spasms a hole in the ground
Continue to suck limes and finger
The hole at the end of their carbines—
Composing epitaphs for everything—

In the tower a bell—silent
For centuries—with no rope
Attached—rings out a note one octave
Below the bird's song—a sound
That estimates then invoices
The heart for the cost of restoring
The light killed by guns.
It is within the context
Of reverence—within the
Fields that are the page—our
Small devotions are hunted
To partial extinction—

Out on the waterless land—
If awake beside a hobbled horse
Late at night beneath a spooky orange
Moon—one hears the ghosts
Of apaches staking out the ghosts of
Conquistadores—smells the stink
Of coven living—rolling between
Whispering stones—the burros

Prodded by children away from the
Incantations of bludgeoned owls—

The end of gaiety in every
Winter rose is such that when

The nursery catches fire it is
The children who rise from the ash
And put it out—

Freeing the spirits waiting for
Another chance to experience
Even a momentary sorrow
Before returning to roost at the end
Of Día de Muertos among
Doves exhausted from carrying prayers
Between variations of silence.

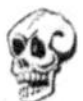

If it were easy to live no
One would wish to die—no one
Alone in the dark with razors
Or pills willing themselves
Away—no one—we'd take our
Chances—and the dead—bless them—
Would be evicted from the organs
Where they get their mail—grow
Stale in the singular company
Of one another like moonshiners
In a small cabin down a dark holler—
Cut off from the world—
Finding everything in family.

But it's hard to live—
Each breath asks for complete
Attention and—when withheld—
The wind is encouraged to shake
The trellis—rattling

The supports—pulling the roses
Apart one petal at a time—

Easier sometimes to die—one
Only has to sip the nectar of a certain
Mirage—fall on a railroad
Spike or drink mezcal while
Climbing the roof to grease a
Squeaking weather vane—endless
Ways to die—to walk to the edge
Of the day and sail off—perhaps laughing
At what waits for a kiss—

A skeleton wanders the narrow
Corridors in the library of breath—
Looking for the books it wrote—

Snake watches the author sleep—
Sees the sherry fumes above its head
Like smoke Lorca would have
Sniffed from his just fired gun—the
Pages darken and turn—darken
And turn even as the author snores
Like a partially paralyzed bugler
Playing "Taps" above an empty hole—

Snake watches the slight
Wind from inaudible curses blow
The pages across the room—
In the night inside the body
They drift like cottonwood
Losing its mind—ignite in midair—
Imagined worlds burning like
Vultures above Popocatépetl.

A fault opens in infinity as if
A posthole digger from the other
Side broke through the emptiness—
Then another small opening—until
The holes meet and a cascade
Of what looks like liquid rubies
Pour from the lips of an old
Wound—spitting light—fire—
Carbon—beginnings—language—
Goats—words—dreams.

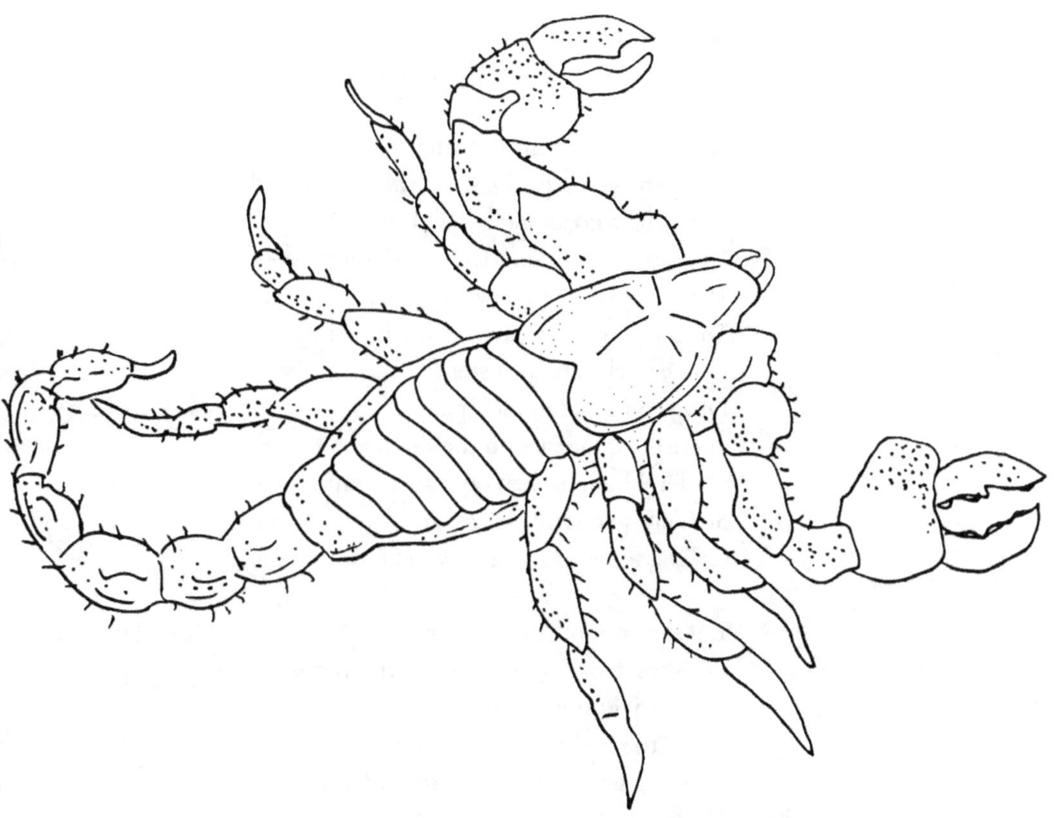

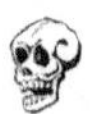

A skeleton sits at a table
Outside a small cantina painted
Blue so long ago it's now the color
Of the merciless summer sky—
Watching the old woman slow—
Then end—her dance—seeing her shawl
Drag in the dust—the sweat on her cheeks
Flowing down the wrinkles made from
Frowning at things retained—

She gathers her dusty rags—leads
The blue roan back to the sky—

When this happens nothing
Happens—except the wind that frightened
The bulls who are no longer bulls—that
Chased the child out from under its bed—
That caused the rope with no bell
To ring—comes to an end the way flies
Come to the end of a stench or a curtain
Drops on a bad monologue—
There are bandages on the shadows
Under which broken bones are healing—
Strident petals on the ground—
Crying for a season that won't return—

The skeleton of this moment
Finishes drinking its cup of bitter herbs—
Bitter to remind it to live again—
Bitter to repel the breath eaters
Looking out of the adobe tower from
The feathered necks of thingadas—

The skeleton watches the old
Woman disappear into it—if not with its gaze
Then with the vestigial habit of gaze—
Wanting in some lymphatic way
To return to the joy—the celebrations
On both sides of the scar—

When the living speak of time they
Imagine a fire ant carrying ice
Into a hole from which the dead
Look out saying—there is no reason
To hurry this gorgeous satisfying
Matter toward a liquid end—
One of the shadows from
The edges of the marketplace
Where *cazadores*—not the living
Ones of course—use knives
To dice the sins from their trigger
Fingers—sits down uninvited
Beside one drunk skeleton who in the
Dazzle of light bouncing from
The pock-marked wall appears to be
Momentarily whole—colored with health
Like the damaged blush of a trampled rose—

This shadow is so bold
As to drink a desperate song
From an empty cup—

In the morning heat it is possible
To see the dead creatures solemnly murmuring
Around the woman wrapped in sheets—

To imagine romance depends not at all
On what expressions a muscle makes

But on mutual trembling after hearts
Are smoked by lust to leather—there is only
One smell left in the broken stones
Of the fallen temple—the sweaty stink of
Neglected gods—and the attar
Of broken bones overpowers it—

Then—like a match held
Inside a sentry's fist—the light
Spills out across the land—

Illuminating—

The wells thick with drowned bees—
Green with solvents that dry to
The color of new currency—the
De nadas rising like metallic
Splatter from a verbal forge—the pages
Stained with honest sombrero sweat—

The old lion at bay—

Hamstrung by invalid shadows—
Monks and chiclet vendors—
The dead on the sideline—wishing
They could prevent what they only
Influence when the lights go out—

The fire in the sentry's fist is a melting igloo
Inside which a cold possibility is thawing
Under the northern lights in each
Predatory eye—burning into movement—
Into a leaf caught to a thin strand of web—
Shimmering from the idea into the action
On its way to breath—the urge to ignite
Overpowered by the thrill of darkening—

Only the dead know how far
The living climb to reach the fruit
They both eat—how the digestion
Of darkness under ground emits
Sunlight up through the leaves
And signals the moon it is time
To disappear from the skulls
Where it has held vigil to enflame
The old notion of growing a new body
Solely from desires that have died—

Everything finds its opposite
Through redemption or struggle—
What isn't complete as it is?

This incandescent glow
That ends the loneliness of another
Fictional day scribbled hastily
By the author before the match
Goes out is the light at the end
Of the narrow point of view shining on
The manure beneath flags and this heavy
Unbearable love that owes nothing
To the living or dead but casts
Its glow throughout every possibility
So the ones awakening in the garden
Between night and day might see
Beyond the languor of the winter rose—

To this place—where everything
Waits breathlessly to arrive.

Epilogue

The blue roan sees the world
As a saddle made of fire—

The reader sees the world
As a grape eaten by purple ghosts—

The vaqueros see the world
Exactly as the world—

El patrón sees the world
As a melting taper with a dinero wick—

The old woman in the trailing shawl
Sees the world as the widow of nothing—

The lost child sees the world
And remains lost by blinking slowly—

The bulls see the world
And snort from a shared incision—

El escorpión sees the world
And sings inside the night wind's horn—

The mirón sees the world
As the insect trapped inside the amber of a lie—

El chingado sees the world
And mistakes his tongue for a worm—

The author sees the world
As a blizzard of medicinal limes—

The living see the world
And hope the scarecrows are real—

The rose sees the world
As the corpse the rain awakens—

The dead see the world
As a matador whose sword is their name—

The world sees itself in the mirror
Of real vaqueros riding dead horses
Tracking fictional bulls between canyons
Where fossils bleed versions of the truth
Downstream to the empty page—

Snake sees the world
In the mucus from a swallowed spear—

The rat sees the world
As an opportunity to reduce a cheese—

The twin boys see the world
As an icon made from genetic tissue—

The game sees the world
As an eye orbiting the sold out seats—

The father sees the world
As a place where his balls made hay—

The poem sees the world
As mountains see an avalanche:

The silence falls into the space
Around the utterance—the grunts

Of fists, the thud of an unshod hoof,
The choir spooked into praise—whisk
Of spattered bull tails the only sound
Other than the dry river's collusion
With shadows—the flies inside the skulls
Trying to imitate a fricative—

The thoughts of the dead
Fall from great heights to the tongue

Of those who speak but are
Afraid of sharing the flowers
Grown behind fenced gardens
Because they are all that's left
Of a seasonal beauty—

Until the gate is broken—
Until cold hands move between
Roses with scissors made of snow—

Until the coins on the eyes of soldiers
And in the hands of merchants
Are of equal value—are lakes
Of pure silver light where the last
Prayer drowns in the silence
From a shrouded face—

Rain collects inside wells
On both sides of a border set
On fire by the burial screams of love—
Now smoking beneath an ancient
Tenderness so much like faith
It hurts when it burns out—

Once there were differences
Between the perception and the moonlight
Glowing on its bloody fur—now
There are only the hidden visions
Within which something lost abides—

Through the window of a new
Moment roses turn red inside of cradles—
Reveal their inner sanctuaries
To the remembered warmth of breath—
Unfold into sunsets that clot like
Clouds in the asters on the mountainside
Above a village entombed by night—

Waiting like desert flowers for a storm
That washes everything away.

Nothing is forgotten—
Nothing is left behind—and no one
Is alone in the days to come.

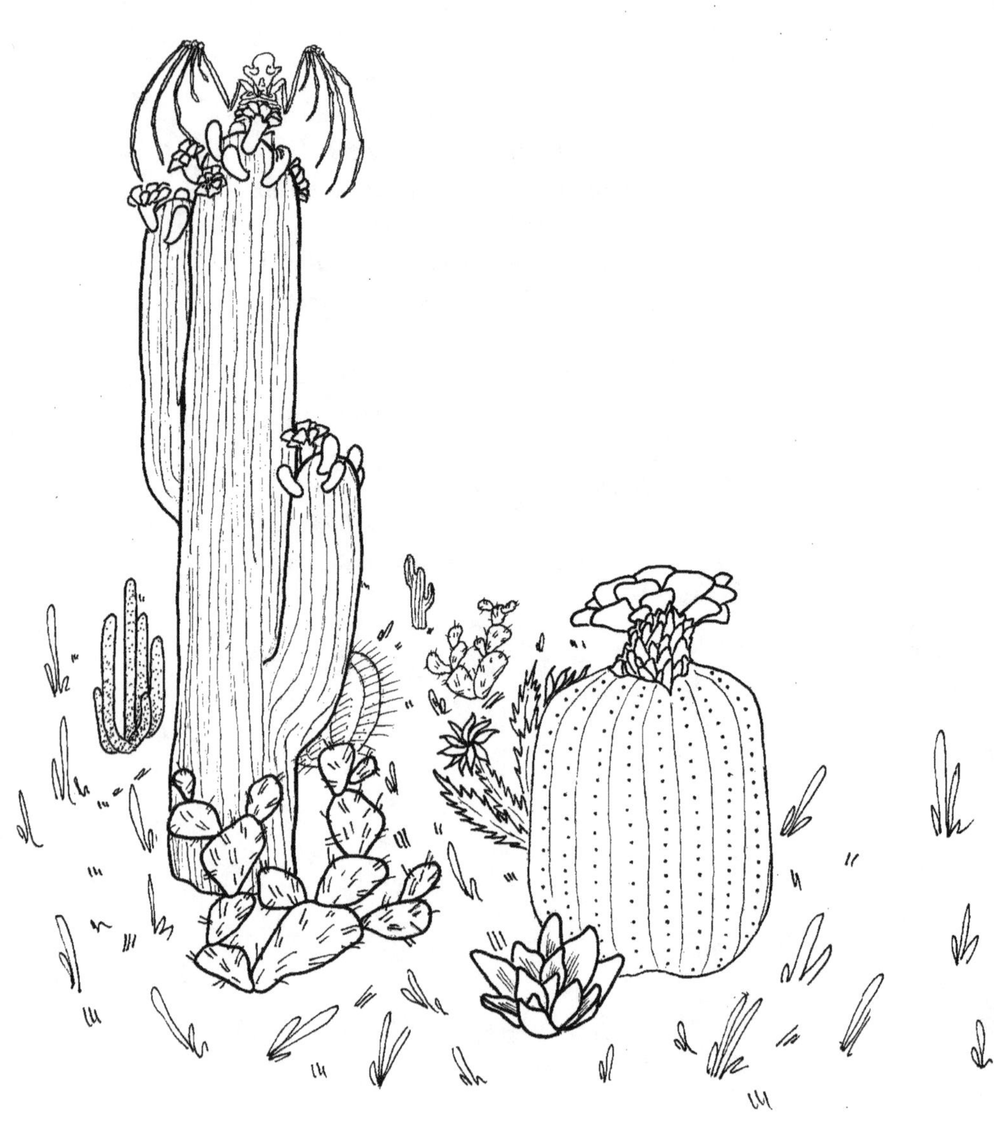

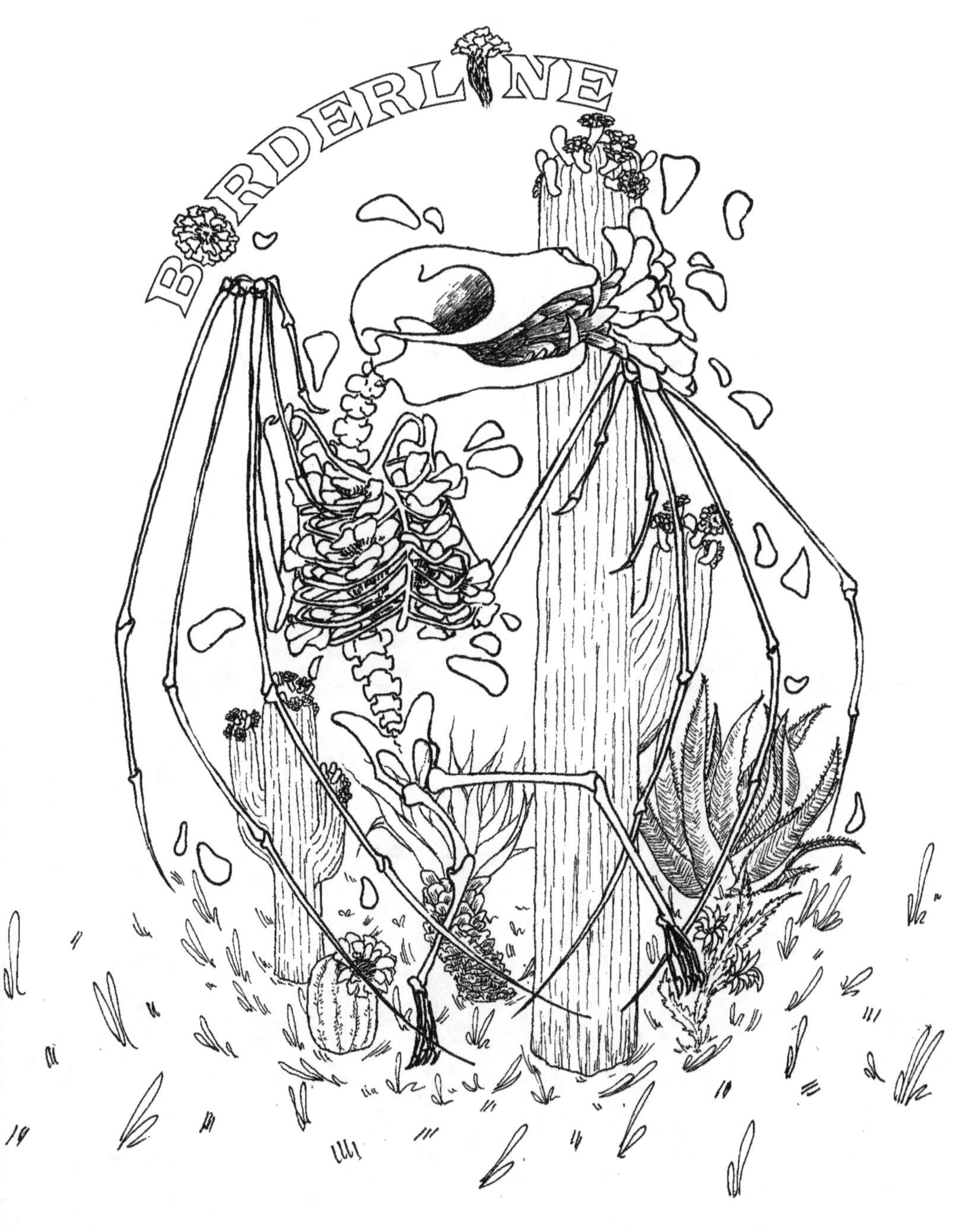
BORDERLINE

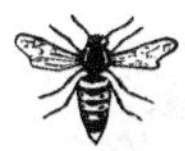

There is something in a bare tree
Looking down at the suffering of everything
Unconcerned it stands out against
The desert sky like a second sun—

Or that its saliva forms a shallow pool
That killed the tree with bitterness—
A place where spiders—then larger creatures—come
To drink—including this elderly hermit—paradise
Bound—who—on bad knees—assuages
Its thirst directly from the mouth of god.

Who looks down from the tree also
Lives in the soles of the feet of pilgrims walking
On hot sand toward an invisible mountain
Glazed by the lauhgter of frozen ghosts—

If we enter here we too walk through
A field of monuments built by earlier
Generations—that is to say—the accomplishments
Of ancestors go unnoticed until—just now—
One who inherited the kingdom
Of all there is uses a cattle prod to
Drive his family up the temple steps
To worship in a place of echoes—

But this is about our shared journey—
Not the borderline between—for that reason
I must chide the saguaro for needling
The blue dawn the queens of the night
Denounce with their slippery pink tongues

And I must remember to whisper
The names of the dead as softly
As sand sucked miles into the sky
Falls back to reshape a dune—

We are jostling one another
In mid dance—suddenly the musicians
Introduce compassion to the music
By accenting a minor note—the tempo changes—and—
With every step—true partnering begins—

Our hands touch another's instrument—
Our tongues lick the same spoon removing
The ant from the soup now that its
Small story has flavored the broth—

One foot after another—the name
Of this hard land chiseled on the heart
Like the epitaph a faithful wife leaves
On the stone of a syphilitic spouse.

The hermit coughs out an
Eye that wanders the hot desert looking
For a place to forget everything it
Sees and especially to forget the way
Strangers in the form of livestock
Eat everything inside a private garden—

The one eyed hermit continues—and yes—
Continues for all of us—the dead as well
As the living—placing a small stone
In its mouth to lubricate the protuberance
Used to spit out prayers.

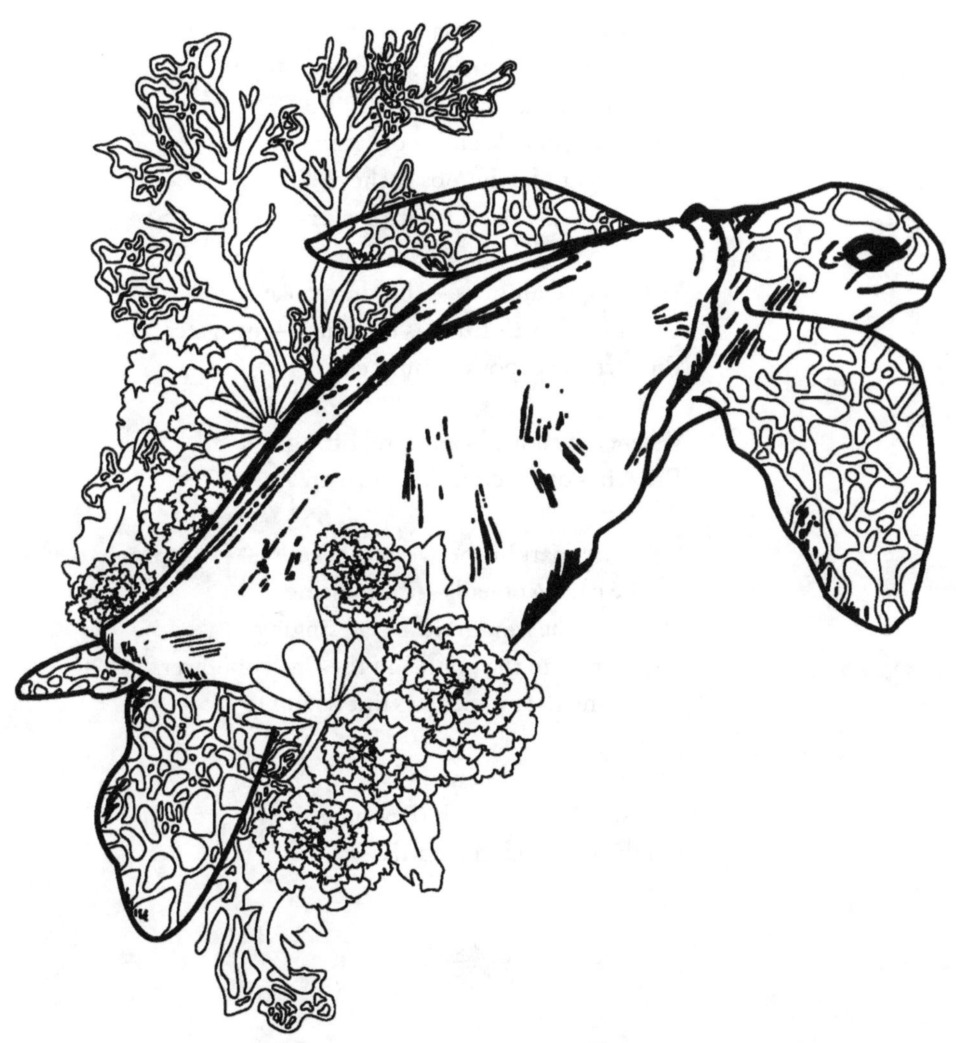

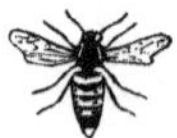

It's the earth rotating in space
That bakes instinct in the oven
Of a swimming shell or sucks moonlight
From a drifting log—brings evil
Out of a cool hole and cooks it in
Noon light like thumbs at the end
Of an arsonist's sleeve—it's a river
Between two banks on fire filled
With singed animals—and the smoke
Coming off their fur—as they sink—instigates
The tornado depositing miracles

Where they don't belong and lifting
The skirts of angels miles downstream—

It's desire sparking between cell walls—
It's the paring of nails—the blessing
Of rain—the iron in the blood singing
To magnets in the earth and the smell of flowers
Indicating the moment a saint begins to rot—

This is the instrument
That sounds best when the swings
On the playground are still.

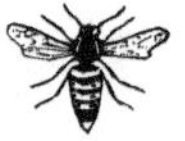

There's great excitement at the edges
Of the mesquite brambles as they watch
The shadows of carrion birds

Pass over the old woman dancing
Inside an interstellar event—

Yes—it's time to reveal the hermit
Is wearing a dress made of something skinned—
Scraped—then softened in its own brain—

Her hair—seen from a distance
As a corona around a grinning skull—
Is backlit by a presumption
The world has codified into an aside
Shouted from behind a spear:

No woman belongs here
Among the grinning thingadas and oozing
Black stingers alone with only a canteen
Filled with the tears of a lost child—

No woman walks through these days
Against the escalators of heroic resolve
Or makes a home in a wilderness
Of slobbering ghouls with only a map
And a sharpened stone—that only bulls
Make dangerous journeys between pastures
Into the hinterlands of myth to drink
From the lake reflecting the setting sun.

Bah!

I forgot to mention her hair is braided
With mouse skulls though it is
Possible nothing said from this point
Is real and we must distrust our eyes—

They are old technology—a cotton gin
Combing the seeds of prophecy from speech—

Exactly who to believe—whose
Poem speaks for the worn out gloves—
Whose story eases thirsty roots in private fields
Where the bulls wander without testicles
Or forage and the sky sizzles like a cigar
Put out in a urinal—whose presence

Casts this shade where the dead
Throw dice for a bendable bone—

The thorn wakes up alert
As a weasel from momentarily
Dreaming its point is dipped
In blood and used to write down
The confessions of a lustful friar
Dragging a cut rope away from the bell
Tower—the white pages of the poem
Transcends the poet's emptiness—

Transcends the legible smear—
Invites the silence of the broken rope
And the fantasies popping out
Like seals beneath the friar's robe—

The back of the empty church
Is in shade and offers a cool hand
To anyone afraid of the bullet holes
In the sunlit adobe walls where
Taggers replicate the execution
With long streaks of red paint—

The desert too waits for the exact
Moment to claim the prize of a soul—
Shimmers its loins suggestively
Until the horizon seems like a hard
Saddle rubbed supple by light.

It waits for the living to come
First on foot and then on knees
And finally face down among ants—

This is the body—our body—no
Matter how many times we enter it—
Or leave it behind—or fall short—
It lengthens before us.

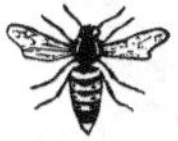

Once I was young enough
To believe where I wandered
In the world was only one step
From hidden bounty and in all directions
The lips of the gods were parted
To receive my tongue—

I came down from the mountains
To enter the small village of San Agustinillo
On the downslope journey to Mazunte
Packing the fugue state of joy
Only the young successfully color
Coordinate with sorrow—

I dig a shallow pit atop an unmarked
Grave—roll a rude cigar and blow smoke
Rings at Saturn—where on the earth
Can one dig without harming a bone—

There are footprints and hoof prints
And evidence of a collective madness
Called grief—depressions in the dirt—
A tear stained cloth—a rosary worn
Down to the hole—a fable in the trees—

A flickering of by tiny blue *thermostats*
With tinier blue tongues—about a great
Battle between giants in the clouds
Come down to earth to suck the leg
Bones off the witnesses—once they
Are cooked—to convince them victory
Over even minor gods is murder.

The village wasn't much maybe
To the world—but to me it was
A holy place to refresh
In quiet and respectful solitude—

Where a colony of caterpillars inside
The trousers of a pale suit thrown
On a thicket of white flowers
Slowly disappears into white flowers
As if grace is a white flower.

I was afraid of everything white
Until all at once the caterpillars
Became indigo birds flying
In circles like galaxies releasing

Forever out of fire—then I lost
My fear of this world and fell asleep
To the lullaby of a blue percussionist
Throbbing in a brown wrist—

The fading ornamental clothing
Of the flowers—the shadow
Of all of this so comfortable it
Took generations to understand
The beauty of enough—or
More precisely—the absence that
Is remarkably always a gift—
I sat down behind an empty church
And fell asleep once again to voices
Saying over and over something like
Leave everything at the door.

(this falling asleep and waking—
over and over—until there is only
the sound of the bell hammered by
time—is the one dream where
it is possible to believe tomorrow
lives not in the bell but in the rope)

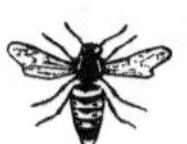

The hermit begins narrating
An interesting version of creation
To the creator—to me this means
She talks to herself and is not looking
For portents in the sand paintings
Made by sunset and wind—rather—
Finds legible joy with her open eyes—

She come down to the village
From her cave in the mountains
To drink salt water in warm tide pools
And to then alter her understanding
Of the importance of listening
To monkeys about the gods
Whose ruined temples are toilets
For bats returning at night to roost
Inside a dark prophecy—

I carried her with me—
Piggybacked—like a prisoner
Carries a precious memory grown
So faint it's possible to lose it
By remembering—or—to accurately describe

The weight of this responsibility—
The feeling of her legs around
My waist is the same as a pinch
Of tobacco welcoming the match—

I bring her with me like
Cupped hands filled with river
Water carried between rows
Of drooping corn—we stoop—

Spines creaking like vultures
Lifting cartilage—looking for gold
That trickled from the vestments
Of conquistadores as they nodded in the shade
Of slaughtered natives—piling bodies

High enough to protect their awful
Armored horses from the sun—

Her ankle length dress is hiked
Above mid-thigh for the utility
Of giving birth to the next moment which
Is a convenience the dead applaud in yellow
From seats inside the husks of corn—

Around her neck is a leathery sack
Filled with crayons to paint the landscape
Wherever it displeases her—

This is a form of prospecting where
Gold is simply a remaining shred of baked
Skin beside a water hole or the gleam
Of teeth inside a smile exposed by wind.

And in the dark night—oblivious
To the dangerous storm driven waves—
The circling sharks—men with hammers
On the shore—she kicks through
The surf—drags her now pulsing shell
Through her broken sisters to arrive.

intermission

we have inadvertently mentioned
a leathery sack and of course the twin
boys from Popul Vuh use this
as a door to enter the poem and brag
once again about the women
in the stands throwing kisses at them
after their great victory over the gods
using the balls left by their father—
even if I could prevent it I wouldn't

try to stop them from telling you
that their manhood began in a stink
of kerosene smoke and mezcal shots
with enraptured women sucking their hands.
and like all victories over the eternal—
only lasted between awakenings.

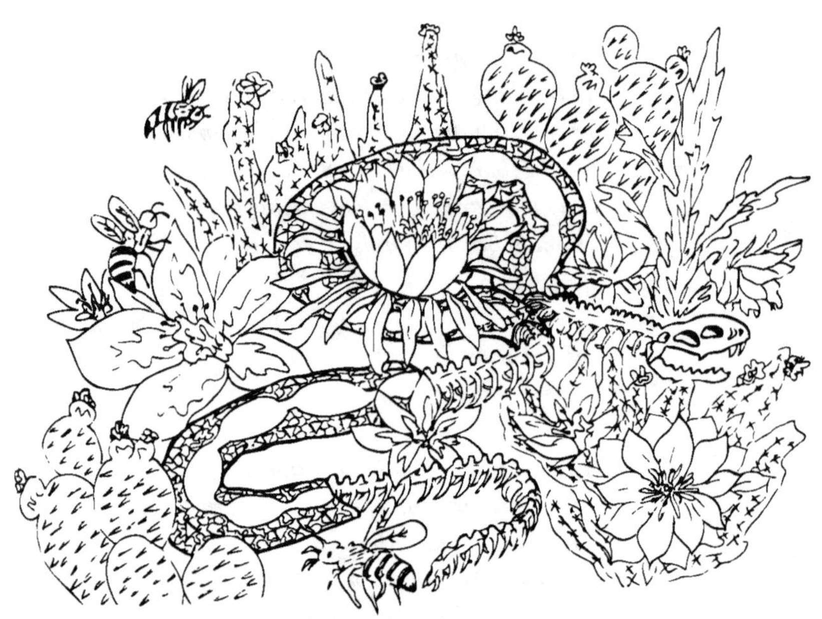

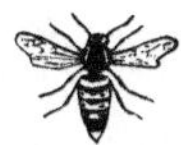

The horse is on its last legs
As a horse though it is impossible
To know how many legs remain
In the endless cycle of lives it has
As rider or as ride—

It stares at the sun
With eyes wet with dreams
No one can interpret but I believe
Relate to a trickle of pebbles initiating
A movement of boulders down the side
Of mountains where they land
In rivers to the detriment of fish.

Sometimes the happiness of journey
Is eclipsed by the happiness it ends.

Behind the huge lashes—like waving
Wheat outlining an inexhaustible
Winter sky—the eyes of the horse
Never blink as the earth fills them.

The forest thins out into grassland
That becomes sand while the rivers
Turn to creeks that dive between
Ribbons of bleached rock
With the skeletons of hellgrammites
Etched like pictographs
On the rotting canyon walls.

Demons would vacation here if they
Weren't already enjoying themselves
So thoroughly atop flagpoles.

One never believes the horizon
Smoking on the edge of vision
Is in truth the future where
Machines drag the sun up
And down stoked by the residue
Of creatures that are like grapes
Between the bare toes of field hands—
That are fuel for bonfires by whose light
Pitchforks remove each fading
Shadow from the burning sand.

I stumble like a wind-up
Toy on the last turn of the key—
Slapping flies with a braided whisk
Made from the mane of the horse—
This electrifies a circle of black
Birds relating the advantages of the aerial
View as they come down for a rib—

Unlike anything I know—except walking
Into a café at the end of a working day
To the smells of fried onions
And the ineffable cheese from cuspidors—
I am astonished to find a waterhole
Underfoot—in a tight crevice
Between two red rocks—just beyond
This visible borderline moonlight

Bleeds from cut flowers that were
Once entire planets for honeybees—

And I am on my knees filling
Two canteens when it touches me—

The little padre with the ammo
Belts around his neck and the pistol
Of his church and the rifle of his atonements
In his smile and his words intended
To teach me the hierarchies
Of abundance in a place of nothing—

He serves only to remind me to spit
Back the small frog as I drink—
With my face buried to the ears—
One gulp before changing kingdoms.

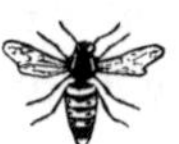

I will give up my chair to the next
Lost soul wanting to sit in the morning sun
Drinking pressed oranges because
I have nested too long for courtesy
In a spot required by those made homeless
From remodeling a personal shrine—

I will leave something behind
And take something away—not just
The torn pant leg or the chapped hands
Or heel worn boots—not just the feel
Of the sand in the moonless night
As the rip tide sizzles and the shell
Lurches out of the sea—

I'll return to another land—
A hole in time—carrying tools between
Jobs and eventually make enough
Ka-ching to come back—if not to this beach
Then to this same chair.

No matter—the world
Struggles to build visible architecture
From the images dug out
Of the eyes of tarantulas tracking

An injured bird—not even
The unblemished though fictional
Fields of snow hold enough light
To make appetite sacred—

In the end—the sun
Goes down and shadows
Merge with night—lending darkness
The extra opacity to consume the solemnity—
The reverence—the faces lit by petitions stuck
On fly strips behind the eyes.

We are all here or there—
Dead or alive—real—as the period
At the end of this
Sentence.

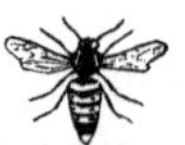

There is always a corner to turn
Into the dim glow of a candlelit hole
Alive with the movement of insects
And the whirring of invisible clocks—

The machinery in the soul
Counts down to the celebration
Where the masks are exchanged
Between soldier in different rags across
Arbitrary lines patrolled by a promise—

Where the hand with no fingers
Holds up a sunset colored blossom
And spirits come out of the ground
To smell themselves in bloom.

The magic bullet and the miracle
Cure are both received when the spectators
Look up from their fists curled around
The handle of a trenching tool
And voluntarily provide the protein
The saguaro needs to survive the nestling
Owls pecking bones in it.

I've walked a thousand miles past
Places like this—the beckoning of gorgons
Masturbating on slippery rocks while sailors
Drown in their eyes—the raw skin
Where the saddle wears down to the song—

The song—the well—the drink—the coast
Where—if one is diligent—it is possible
To become a driftwood flower.

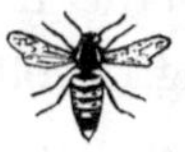

There's something in a satchel
Waiting to explode—there's something in the shed

In the dark corner near the cool
Earth behind a shovel—waiting—
There's kindness granulated out of love
Standing on a rotten bridge—waiting—

There's a moist path in all directions
That leads to a great dryness—there's a goat bleating
At the end of a tether—there's a child
Looking up from a bucket unable to slap
A mosquito on its mother's breast—

There's goodness in the heart
Of mountains under snow waiting
For evening to silence the goat—

There's men in panties who pull
Empires down—there are women who hate
These men—women who love these
Men and men who love these men but where
Are the women who love the women
Who oppose these men—

There's a nail in a tire on a vehicle
In the passing lane—there's of course roses dying
In glorious splendor above the long buried
Unread works of Rafael Guillén Vicente—

There's a burro on the menu—a glimpse
Of hope in the bathroom mirror—there's creatures
Working together to come apart—there's
Love pushing a stroller with pumpkins in it—
There's no reason to look anywhere—
There's the feeling this is all
A lie even as the beatification of yesterday
Produces a dark but edible fruit—

There's someone snorkeling in the blood
With a spear gun and the bends—there's
No reason to run from that long shadow—

It begins again and ends
Again in the cold swelling— The upwelling of blue waves into black sky
Into the white light of the moon—

The bones inside the skin move
The heart—the sand under the sea
Speaks to the sand on the shore—
We are coming—we are here—

Dragging the future
Into the light long enough
To see it deliver a sunset
Is no way to create an interesting
Biography but nonetheless
I am dreaming while the world
Falls in pieces around me—these pieces—
These tomorrows—stirred by instinct
And alive inside a temporary eye—

In the dirt rectangle under the sun
Bleached awning above the plastic chairs
The owner of the cantina is slapping
A bartender with his rolled up hat
While a one eyed cat dismantles
A brightly colored parrot in the weeds
Near the foundation of what
Is agreed to be existence—

I thumb the cork back into
The bottle of mezcal without taking
My first sip of the day with the sun

A red boil about to burst
Through the dusty green foliage
Above the village—from the limp
Jungle all the way down to the coast—
A smile is spreading through the air
In anticipation of the moment the blue
Sky is summarized completely
By the book the waves just finished
And delivered like a first edition
To the shore—where creatures
Wanting—like everything wants—to live
Swim into this story so exhausted
They carry nothing but a single heavy breath
And the epitaph for silence floating
Like the mezcal worm in their blood—

I could fall asleep right now.
I too have traveled beyond my abilities
To places where my presence
Threatens the inhabitants—stranded
In the same conscience of an intoxicated
Cleric peeking at the cleavage of a nun—

It is not enough to placate
The gods with postponements
Of essential disrespect—though
They may not exist—even so—
The wrath of fictional characters
Is capable of becoming as real
As the twin eyes of a serpent
Coiled inside a wanderer's boot.

For this reason only
I uncork the bottle

To properly grieve for the parrot
Whose blue and red feathers

Flutter in the dirt while its
Screams turn into a lyrical rain
The wind blows back out to sea.

Epilogue

In between two half truths
The ocean thunders—the force of waves
Sucks down the moon and regardless
Of what truth is believed or the sermons
Wrapped inside burlap bags
In the trunks of limousines or desert
Poets lecturing thorns—

There's no place where light
And dark don't press their flesh
Together like new lovers taking
Pleasure without exchanging vows
Or names—erasing the lines between
Them—the simple differences of degrees—
With the ecstasy of the dead whispering
To drunkards in a burning car.

The thing doesn't know it occurs
On both sides of a fundamental line—

Turning corners on a dark street
Beneath a blue bug light—the thing is running
Through zapped insects that crunch
Like shells used to pave a road—

The thing avoids steel in the hands
Of a bearded child—the thing is disguising
Forever its history as a nail—the thing
Is drinking the see of the sea—the thing
Is leaving bones in the sky and runs when
Hearts stopped by shared guilt leave
Roses where the gardener falls—
The thing grows a rib from a cry
For help—the thing holds another thing
While another thing emerges from a dream
And briefly plays in traffic—the thing
Grooms in a puddle—the thing breaks
An E string to improve the music—

The thing is fighting free of the sea—
Out of the flesh—inland—into the clock
Ticking in the coconuts—the thing is using
Its face to chip gold from a cradle—

When we are alive it is possible
To die by our own hand but what is less
Commonly known is the dead
Commit suicide by choosing to live again.

It's not yet morning—the owls
Are tiring in the purple gray light
As the last of their prey moves underground—
They are flying back to the saguaro
With bits of creatures for their young—

I too see the day is about to begin—
The night end—the world stop—
While one unexpected instant
Of tenderness and fearsome disorder
Helps everything on both sides

Digest the trickle of ancient light
Still pulsing from original fire that
Announces this shared earth is where
We extract from silence our perfect song.

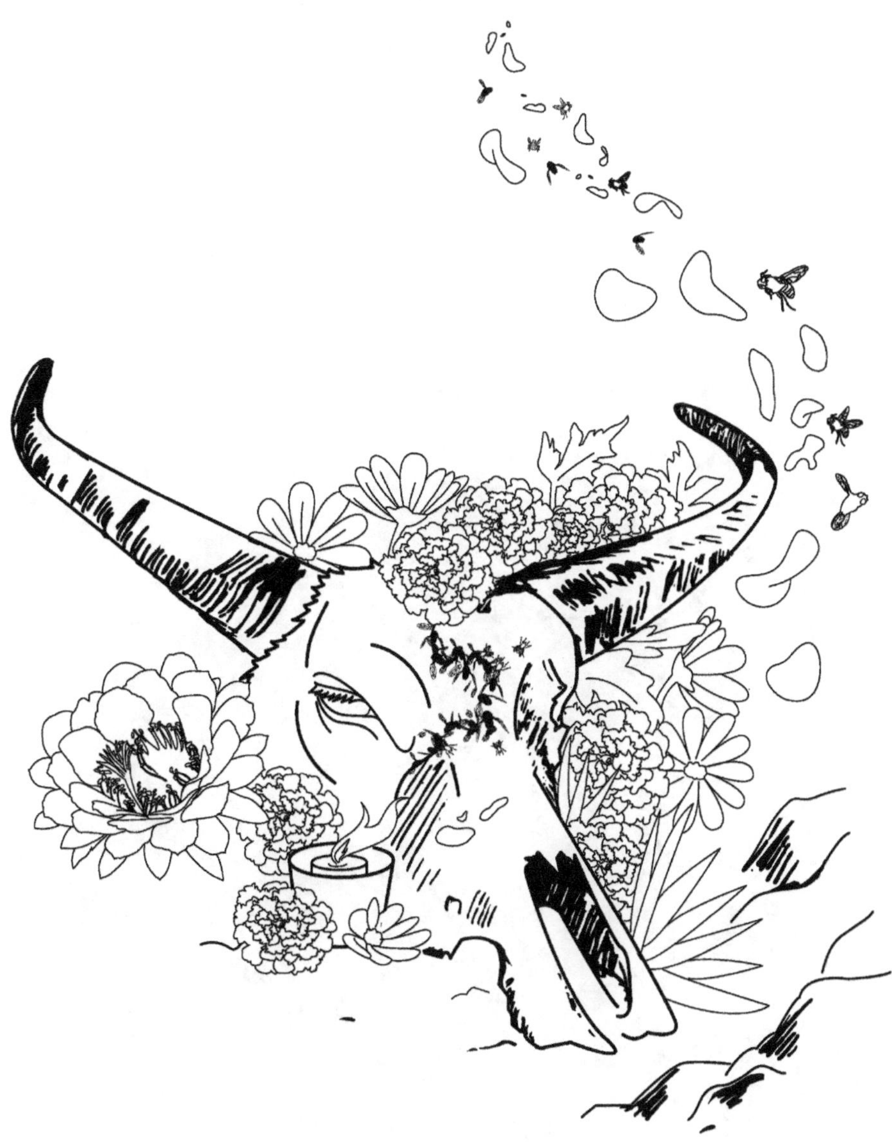

www.ingramcontent.com/pod-product-compliance
Lightning Source LLC
LaVergne TN
LVHW010628100826
845148LV00014B/3160

9781597097345